Pendulum

How to Use Truth Testing for Clarity and Peace of Mind

(Tips and Tricks to Unlock Your Inner Magic and Enhance Your Life)

Published By **Bengion Cosalas**

Evelyn Ross

Pendulum: How to Use Truth Testing for Clarity and Peace of Mind (Tips and Tricks to Unlock Your Inner Magic and Enhance Your Life)

ISBN 978-1-77485-646-8

Legal & Disclaimer

The information contained in this ebook is not designed to replace or take the place of any form of medicine or professional medical advice. The information in this ebook has been provided for educational & entertainment purposes only.

The information contained in this book has been compiled from sources deemed reliable, and it is accurate to the best of the Author's knowledge; however, the Author cannot guarantee its accuracy and validity and cannot be held liable for any errors or omissions. Changes are periodically made to this book. You must consult your doctor or get professional medical advice before using any of the suggested remedies, techniques, or information in this book.

Upon using the information contained in this book, you agree to hold harmless the Author from and against any damages, costs, and expenses, including any legal fees potentially resulting from the application of any of the information provided by this guide. This disclaimer applies to any damages or injury caused by the use and application, whether directly or indirectly, of any advice or information presented, whether for breach of contract, tort, negligence, personal injury, criminal intent, or under any other cause of action.

You agree to accept all risks of using the information presented inside this book. You need to consult a professional medical practitioner in order to ensure you are both able and healthy enough to participate in this program.

Table Of Contents

Chapter 1: What is Dowsing, and how do I get it?

Before we start to talk about pendulum, dowsing, you need to be familiar with the basics of dowsing. The majority of people have never heard or seen dowsing before. While dowsing may seem like a fascinating hobby, you can expect to find a world of divination you've never seen before.

Often referred to as divining, the practice of dowsing allows you to locate anything underground. For example, one could use dowsing in order to locate underground water or minerals, metals, ores, metals gemstones, oil, and gravesites. It is also possible to use Dowsing for searching for answers to unanswered questions.

Pendulum dowsing isn't something that's very popular in modern times, but it has been practiced for centuries. It is believed that the practice originated from Germany in the 15th and 16th centuries. Martin Luther's 1518 proclamation which described dowsing in metals as an act defying the first commandment was one of the first known mentions of dowsing.

People who didn't know the force behind dowsing have been afraid of it throughout history. Although it was initially thought to be a criminal practice, many who were afraid of the practice admit they didn't know how it actually worked.

Germans used the dowsing approach to locate metal ore underground by the mid-1500s. German mining technology eventually became so popular that it was in high demand all over Europe. German miners moved to Elizabethan England because of their success. There they lived and worked very well.

South Dakotan farmers practiced dowsing to find water sources within their farms as early as the 20th century. Homesteaders and ranchers also used dowsing. In fact, some of them still use it today. During Vietnam War, United States Marines actually used the dowsing method to locate weapons or tunnels. The Norwegian army used dowsing methods in 1986 to locate soldiers who had been lost in the avalanche caused by a NATO drill Anchor Exec. This was just 30 years old. Although scientists are not able to explain the whys of dowsing in detail, their use has been proven successful throughout history.

Many prominent figures from history have supported the art and practice. General Patton, Robert Boyle (a distinguished scientist), Charles Richet (1999 Nobel Peace Prize winner) and Leonardo da Vinci were all supporters of pendulum dosing.

Perhaps the best thing about dowsing, is its ability to find anything that has been lost. This includes pets, objects, people and even people. The search for a lost dog by a couple was made possible in the early 1990s using dowsing. Also, dowsing can be used to search out archaeological remains.

Pendulum dowsing helps people find lost items and hidden objects underground. But, others believe the pendulum could provide answers to daily questions. This is what we will discuss in the next chapters. No matter your intention, your pendulum practice can lead to some amazing discoveries and unexpected information.

While some believe those with predisposed psychic abilities will be able to dowse best, many dowsers insist that anyone can do it. As with all supernatural practices, it's best to let dowsing develop naturally. Dowsing is not something you can control. You must let it happen.

Some people take up dowsing as a hobby and seem to have an inborn gift. It is almost as if the person seeking dowsing leads them to everything. Others attempt to do dowsing but fail repeatedly. Don't get discouraged with dowsing.

While some dowsers might be more gifted than others it can be learned. With patience, openness, and the willingness to learn, you will be able dowse and find hidden treasures, artifacts, or other items that others may not have thought of. Although the guide will primarily focus on pendulum and other methods of dowsinging, you can also use them in other ways. We will first go over the basics. The next chapter will focus on how to begin your own pendulum practice.

Chapter 2: Preparing for Pendulum Dowsing

A pendulum is something you've likely seen before. However, you may not have known it could be used in tapping into unknown bodies of water or artifacts. The pendulum is most commonly associated with cartoons and would be used by hypnotists in order to encourage patients into meditative or sleep-like states. Pendulums can be used as a point of reference, but they also have other, much more impressive powers.

It falls so far under the category "unknown" that Albert Einstein even lauded its amazingness. Einstein, perhaps among the greatest physicists ever, believed strongly in the authenticity. He also stated that dowsing shows the response of the human nerve system to certain factors that are unknown at this time. Decades later, it is still difficult to tap into those unknown variables.

Einstein believed that the magnetic energy of electromagnetic energy was capable of causing the pendulum to turn. It makes perfect sense. Radios can picks up signals from radio waves, which cannot be seen. Why wouldn't an instrument like a pendulum be able receptive other, unseen energies. Energy creates vibrations and waves. People, places, objects, and all things are made up of it. Perhaps the science behind a pendulum is still being developed. It's possible it won't be fully understood. It is still possible to use it for our own benefit, and practice using it frequently.

To start, you will need a pendulum. Some people create their own pendulums. Pendulums are actually just weights suspended from a non-magnetic rod or string. Pendulums can be made of any type of material, including a paperclip attached with cotton thread. However many people prefer to purchase a peduncle or use an actual weight on the string. Pendulum weight material that is popular with beginners is brass. This makes it easy to buy these types online before you start your practice.

You should also acquire a pendulum graph before starting your practice. Although you can purchase a more detailed pendulum chart, this guide will show you how to use it. This guide will teach you how to use it. You can also see the chart below.

Once you have your chart and pendulum, you can begin your first practice in quiet surroundings. It's best to be completely alone in order to avoid any distractions. It's important that you choose a spot which you are able to return regularly to. This will allow for you to return the same spot often, which is very beneficial for those just starting to learn how to Dowse.

Even if you're already familiar with someone who does dowsing, you might find it helpful to go along with an experienced one for your first attempt. Some novice dowsers report greater results because they can harness the energy of an experienced one.

Before you do dowsing it is essential to fully relax. Let your mind and breathing relax, allow your spirit to flow freely, and let your mind rest. Before you begin dowsing, don't feel stressed or weighed down. It is okay to meditate on a regular basis to help you feel more relaxed and at ease before you start dowsing.

Once you have relaxed completely, take your pendulum and keep it close to the string. The string should pass between your thumbs. Between your fingers and weight, there should be approximately 1/2 to 3-inches of string. The string length dictates the swing speed, so pay attention to that as you watch the swing.

Keep the pendulum pointing at your chart. You may either use the chart shown on the previous pages or make your own.

Now, you can hold the pendulum by your fingers and use your hand to guide it. The pendulum will begin swinging in the direction marked "YES" on a chart. Without you directing the swing, ask the pendulum for its permission to keep going towards the yes. For beginners it is crucial to express your request. Use a normal, conversational voice.

If the pendulum is not moving, stop it from moving and ask it to go on. Concentrate only on the upper (or forward-moving) half of the pendulum's swing. You should pay no attention whatsoever to the swinging pendulum. The process can be repeated until the swing continues on its' own. The purpose of this exercise is to make the pendulum swing by itself, without your intervention.

After you've finished that step you'll go back to the beginning and repeat the same procedure for the word NO. You will still need to hold the pendulum straight over the center circle of the chart. Continue to ignore half the swing just as you did the "YES" motion.

This is not the time to be discouraged. Even though you may not be successful, the pendulum might not swing automatically the first time that you try. Consider taking a break if you're not having success.

After the pendulum starts swinging toward the "NO," you can ask it to continue its journey clockwise towards reaching the "YES."

The pendulum must continue to be "Ready for Question." You can ask it to do this vocally.

After the pendulum moves in a clockwise direction, you can ask it for a counterclockwise movement. It will move from the "Ready To Ask" direction to the "YES", then onto the" NO, and back again.

This is because you will have to practice these steps multiple times before you become comfortable using the pendulum. Always start with the Yes and keep going in the same order as the above.

Chapter 3: Using Your Pendulum

Your pendulum is available in several different ways. Programming it is vital, especially if the purpose of your pendulum is to help you answer any questions you may have. Below, we'll be discussing programming your pendulum.

The previous chapters will help you to master the fundamentals of pendulum dosing. Program your pendulum first.

Your pendulum should begin swinging in the direction of "Ready for Question". Only then you can ask your Pendulum a question. It is essential to start your question with "May", or "Can", or "Should."

If it swings towards "NO", you should stop. This does not mean that the pendulum can't be used at all. It simply means that the pendulum won't work for the user until a later moment. Keep it in your possession.

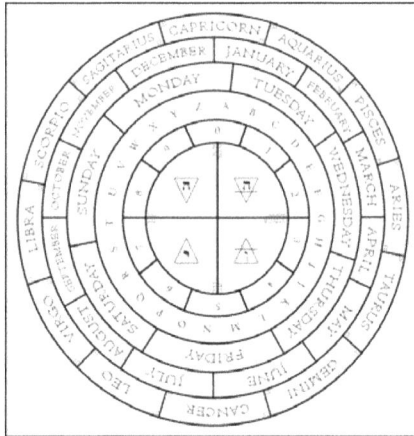

If however the pendulum swings towards "YES", you may continue with a program. Individual programs are possible, but all programs will outline the purpose for a person's Dowsing practice. The program typically describes the purpose of a person's dowsing practice. This includes their intentions, influences. time frames, and methods of answering. If you don't know much about dowsing, you can find a program online or at a meeting. Many dowsing societies have chapters that meet regularly all over the globe.

Once you are done reciting your programme, you will just say, "End the program." We appreciate your cooperation.

It's also necessary to conduct a final inspection, where you ask your pendulum if the conditions are acceptable. Before moving on, ensure it swings towards the "YES".

Once you have followed these steps, you will be able program your pendulum. This will ensure that you do not need to repeat the steps each time your pendulum turns on.

Each program will have specifics that include clear directions and agreements. It is important to ensure that your practice is clear. Your subconscious plays an important part in your dowsing practices when you use the pendulum as a tool to answer questions. While the pendulum's answers may not be accurate if you skip programming, it can increase your practice's legitimacy by completing all steps.

Once your pendulum is programmed, you are ready to start asking it questions. Begin with questions that do not matter to you. They should not have any emotional or societal significance. For example, it would be foolish to ask about where a missing item is located that you consider to be extremely valuable. You may instead want to inquire about a vitamin/nutrient level in your body.

As you answer more complicated questions, you may need a more detailed diagram of the pendulum. These can be printed online or ordered by experts. You will learn to use your message charts and how to read them. You might find that your message chart can be used to communicate spiritual messages.

After asking inconsequential samples questions, you should perform a final verification before continuing. If you want to make sure your questions are answered, first ask your pendulum to move clockwise toward the lower circle. Ask your pendulum what percentage of the results were affected by your feelings. Some beginners may find their influence greater than that of experienced dowsers. Regular use of your pendulum will help you build trust in your dowsing practices. This will give you greater success because the answers are more authentic and less influenced by your personality.

Finally, after getting used to the pendulum every day, you may want to ask it if it's okay for you to return the primary program. If it replies yes, you can go back to the primary program. If it replies "NO," it means that it has been properly programmed. In this case, you can change or enter other programs. You can now ask your pendulum all questions. You can have immeasurable knowledge by having faith and trusting your device. This will help you find the answers you are looking for.

Chapter 4: Enhancing Your Pendulum Practice

You've learned the basics of programming your pendulum as well as how to ask it questions. Pendulum dowsing encompasses much more than what we've already covered. We'll now give you some helpful tips to make your practice more efficient and enjoy rewarding results with your pendulumdowsing.

First, be cautious in the way that you formulate your questions. While it is easy to believe that your pendulum might be malfunctioning, there are instances when you could actually be wrongly framing your question. If, for instance, you ask if the dog requires food, the answer will always come back "Yes." Even though you have probably fed the dog all day, the dog needs food every day. This means that regardless of how much food you've given your dog, the answer is always "yes".

You should be aware of unintentional conflicts. The dowsing technique works very literally. You need to be more specific than what you think is necessary. Asking questions may require you to include variables that you don't consider significant. But in reality, this will help you get the right answer. You can pretend you're talking to someone new who doesn't know much about your situation. Instead of asking, "Will I get married to my brother?" instead, you could ask, "Will William be married by December 31st?"

It is crucial that your questions provide clear, factual answers. For example, the dowsing software cannot answer an opinion-based inquiry. Your question must give you a definitive, real answer. This means that you would not ask the pendulum whether your spouse feels happy. "Happy", however, is a relative term and can refer to different people.

Let's look at a concrete example to show you what you might face when using your pendulum. Perhaps you are searching for water nearby. A pendulum might ask you "Is it possible to get water near my home?" It may seem like a sensible question to you but it's better not to be too literal. Instead, ask: "Is it possible to find water in the area (state specific)?" This will allow you to determine the best spot to drill a new well.

You might even wish to program your pendulum by using a particular water program. The internet and dowsing societies have instructions that will assist you with programming. If you are doing an on-site survey, your pendulum needs to point out the exact location and source of water after you have asked it the question. Edge-ofproperty do dowsing will allow you to find the correct direction.

Chapter 5: Map Dowsing and Other Tips

Pendulum Dowsing can be performed at any location to locate hidden gems or buried artifacts. However, it is possible to locate these items even without ever stepping foot on the actual area. Map dowsing allows this to be done. A map can be used to locate the location of your target object. Instead of having to physically travel to that area and dowse onsite, This is especially beneficial if your location isn't clear. With a scaled-down map, you can cover more area. It can be very useful if the item you're searching for is far from your home. Map dowsing can help you pinpoint the location of your desired item so you don't have to search for it when you get there.

Some dowsers opt to use map-dowsing rather than onsite drowsing. Even though this method is still somewhat mysterious, many dowsers swear by its effectiveness. Instead of having to physically do the dowsing at the site or in close proximity, some dowsers can locate the object, water source and other information they are looking for by dowsing across a map.

Map dowsing can be best for advanced dowsers. You can however give it a shot by following the steps below.

First, you'll require a straightedge. Move it from left-to-right across a plan. Ask your question by using the "May II," "Can I", or "Should II" approach. Ask your Pendulum to indicate when your straight edges have approached your target. This is, in other words: when your straight edges intersect with the area that the item you're searching for can be found.

If your pendulum keeps swinging toward the "YES", it will indicate that you are on target. You can check the chart in this eBook to see if your pendulum has been moving in the right direction while you are near your target.

The pendulum should always swing directly above the "YES." If it does, it will be too far to the right. You can trace the straight edge with a pencil if the pendulum's swing is over the "YES."

Then go vertically again, making sure your straight edge runs up-and/down, instead of horizontally across the pages. Ask your pendulum again to indicate the exact location of your target. Pay attention to where it hits the letter "YES." That is when your vertical line can be drawn.

The point at which two lines intersect is where you will find your target.

No matter which method you choose to use your pendulum in, always keep wind direction in mind as you do your practice. The outcome of your practice can be dramatically affected by the wind direction.

Programming can be as individualistic, as you'd like. If your goal is only to ask "yes/no" questions, then you can request that your pendulum spin in a clockwise/counterclockwise direction via programming. This will indicate a "yes/no" response. This is especially useful if your goal is to locate something while you're out in the open, and/or if there's wind.

Some people don't like the idea of dowsing. It can attract all kinds of energy, even negative ones. You don't have to worry about being attracted to negative energies. Your mind can be directed to stay detached and your mind will not interfere with your practice. You can also communicate with your dowsing instrument as if you were speaking to a person. This ensures that all energies will go to your dowsing instruments and not to the person you are. It allows you instead of being too spiritually invested in your practice of dowsing, to be able to objectively examine the responses.

Remember to ask the "May," "Can", or "Should", questions. If your instrument gives a negative response, you should follow its lead. Your pendulum is unlikely to respond to your desire to alter someone's karmic power, for example. It is not wise to try to change someone's karma. Avoid doing things that your pendulum warns to you against.

Pendulum dowsing provides a wealth of untold information. However, it is crucial that you are respectful of other people's privacy. Some individuals have the ability to shield themselves from these interferences. However, others don't know this. Some people are easy to exploit. Be careful not to look into other people's business. While the pendulum is a tool that you can use for your own advantage, it should never be used in the wrong direction.

It is tempting to depend on your pendulum in order to find answers to all aspects of your life as you grow your dowsing knowledge. Pendulum dowsing, while a powerful method to find lost objects and items, answer unanswered inquiries, and even pass your time, should not be considered an authority. Pendulums should not be trusted with medical diagnoses. A trained physician should be consulted if someone you know has a medical problem.

Keep your mind open to dowsing. While it can be beneficial to allow your mind to flow freely while you do your practice, it is important that you learn to not let your thoughts and feelings impact the outcome. A common mistake made by beginners is to desire a specific outcome, or to influence the response of the pendulum. You won't be benefited by this. Instead, think about new ideas and concepts in a neutral, open way. You can't let your preconceived notions or beliefs hold you back from exploring a new world. Be open to the practice, but don't complicate it by having a lot of opinions and rules. The world of pendulum and dowsing will give you the opportunity to open your mind.

What exactly is a pendulum?

A pendulum can be described as a small, weighted object that is attached and suspended by a string (or a chain). The object can be used to divinate purposes by the person who holds it. Pendulums can be connected to the subconscious by the person holding the string, chain or string. When small movements in the arm cause the pendulum's swing to occur, the pendulum will respond to these movements. According to the "dowsing" of pendulum users, the swing's direction can be attributed to the user answering questions. This is possible thanks to the "dowser" having established a base vocabulary in relation with the movements. The base language allows for specific answers such as YES/NO.

Dowsing describes items that can be used for divination. This includes divining rods, pendulums, and divining sticks. Other items that a "dowser," such as a radio antenna or extended radio antenna, can be used as extensions to one's intuitive abilities. Many dowsers are skilled at using tools such an oblong branch or two metal rods called 'L' rods. They can dowse for precious metals, oil, and water.

Water dowsers, also called "water witches", were hired in the early 20th centuries to aid farmers with their decisions about where to drill their water wells. However, dowsing existed before the term "Water Witching", which became a popular name, was coined. Cave drawings from before 6000 BC, which predate the Bible, show images of what could only possibly be called a Dowsing Rod.

Over a thousand years later, dowsing has become a popular practice in Europe. The most notable example was in 15th-century Germany where the emergence of new eras in dowsing occurred during a time when many villages in desperate need of fresh water. Unfortunately, this was at the same period that the Catholic Church condemned any esoteric activity as "of God" or "of evil."

The benefits of dowsing to improve the lives of others far outweighed any "devil's influences" in the eyes many priests or bishops. Thus, many men of God began using dowsing techniques to help villages find water and plan their crops. However, God did not approve of this practice.

As society developed and became more open-minded, dowsing became more common even though it still retains a magical air. Yet, dowsing remains popular and is especially popular in France where doctors still use pendulums.

Please remember that dowsing can be used for more than just divination. Dowsing allows you access to hidden memories or forgotten thoughts in your subconscious. You can also access the infinite knowledge stored within the universal awareness, which is our link to all knowledge around the universe. Technologically, dowsing is similar to searching the Internet for information.

Pendulums, which can also be used for dowsing, act as metal detectors. They function as homing device to search the ground for any material the dowser wants to locate. You might have read some of my Blueprint books. The central theme of Blueprint is "intend".

Since I was ten years of age, I have been reading numerous books about the study or the use of the pendulum.

The pendulum connects you to your higher self at the core. You can use any small weighted object suspended on a string such as a ring tied with a piece, of floss, or a penny taped or purchased online.

There are many different types of pendulums. They include wooden bobs with polished gemstones or copper pendulums. Witness pendulums include hollowed pockets. This allows the dowser a sample from the source material that they are dowsing to be kept in the pendulum. A dowser seeking oil might add a drop to the pendulum, or place a small oil vial in the hollowed central of the pendulum. This will serve as witness to the dowser before they begin dowsing hundreds of acres of land for the best locations to drill for oil.

Personally, I do not believe you need to have a witness to search the ground for oil, water and gold. I believe your "intention to search" for oil is just like using a witness. My other Blueprint books will tell you that "intent" plays a significant role in the concepts of my series.

Before we get started, a pendulum will be needed. You can have your wedding ring on a necklace, or attach a penny to a piece or string. If you're not sure which type of pendulum is right for you, I suggest you search the internet for "Pendulum" and "Dowsing Pendulum." The following websites are even better:

1. Pendulums.com for double pyramid pendulums.

2. 7dayalchemicalrings.co for manifestation pendulums.

3. Amazon.com offers many sizes and shapes in gemstone pendulum necklaces as well as keychain pendulums.

4. Unseenhandz.com John the Conquerer Root pendulums

All four websites have the different pendulums I use.

Pendulums have many uses. They can help you to make crucial decisions, identify lost items, look for car keys that are misplaced, detect oil and water, and even help you with harmful substances such EMF and carbon monoxide. Pendulums are also useful as energy healing tools and as manifestation tools in similar ways to my books The Energy Healing Blueprint, The Law of Manifestation Blueprint, or The

Pyramid Energy Blueprint. These books cleanse your auric fields and help you manifest your desired outcomes.

There are so many ways that a pendulum can help you live a better life. It's amazing that someone could use a small suspended object to detect hidden objects. It is possible with a pendulum. You can "tune" into your subconscious thoughts to gain new information.

Pendulums are as compact, simple, and intuitive as any other tool. You are always ready to "tune-in" to the correct answers wherever you go. Your pendulum can be carried around in your pocket, worn as an ornament, or attached to a keychain.

Because I don't know when I will need it, I carry a Pendulum with my every move. Furthermore, it strengthens the connection between you and your pendulum.

In the spirit of sharing my own experience, let me tell you how I came across dowsing.

You will understand and appreciate how pendulum dowsing could change your life.

MY EXPERIENCES with the PENDULUM

Pendulums were first introduced to me at ten years old when I was in line at the grocery counter with my mother. I used to be bored of being dragged around the store and waiting for my mom's checkout. However, instead of looking at the booklet rack with 25-30 page booklets about every topic you could think, including books on crocheting, dog grooming. Fortune telling, crockpot cooking, weight loss secrets, and beauty tips. But this particular day was something else.

Out of all the adult subjects included in these booklets I finally noticed one. I was immediately enthralled by the small booklet, which had a pendulum printed on its cover. I thumbed through the book, and I was even more excited to read, "The pendulum is a tool which unlocks every hidden and gives you the exact solution to any question."

I begged Mom to buy it. Given my curiosity, she was easily persuaded and I walked out the store holding a new booklet. Soon, I would have the ability to answer all of my questions. I'd know which girls I liked at school. I would know ahead of time if I was going in for the basketball team. I would know where I could catch most fish. I would know where the railroad tracks are located so I could cash them out to make more money for the community pool.

We returned to the house and, as soon as all the groceries were gone, my mother and me read our pendulum booklets together. She quickly helped me make my very first pendulum. I used a penny that was attached to a piece on string. After teaching me the basic YES/NO movements in the booklet, I was ready to go. I made a simple graph YES/NO, and began asking each question that came to me.

Mom was there to keep an eye on me to make sure my pendulum skills were developing. The pendulum was a game that we played together. I used my pendulum as a homing device or metal detector to locate her car keys, which she would place somewhere in the house.

Within a matter weeks, I had become very skilled in using my pendulum to locate her keys. I also invented a pendulum strategy for my phone that I named "Who's calling?". My phone would ring and I'd quickly ask my Pendulum who was calling.

Who's calling?

Mandy is your cousin? Pendulum swings NO

Keith, is this your friend? Pendulum swings NO

Is that my grandma? Pendulum swings YES

"Hello grandma," i said, picking up my phone.

"Ian. How did I know it was you?" she asked.

"My pendulum told me..."

Although I fell for using my pendulum, it was not my first love. I soon became distracted by other things, and my love faded. Then one day, while staying at my grandmother's house, I was flicking through The National Enquirer's gossip magazine and came across an advertisement that looked bizarre. It was a picture displaying a chart and a board. It was similar to a Ouijaboard but more elaborate. The Pyramid Energy Blueprint is my previous book. You might remember this story. This incredible chart had the alphabet, the numbers 1-9, crosslines to indicate YES and NO and even a pyramid that could be used to "charge" your pendulum for more accurate readings. I was able get mine for $19.99

The pendulum was too expensive for me so I had to order it. I made my pendulum chart using cardboard and the image in my ad. I used my grandmother's coffee containers to draw circles. Then I used a straightedge line ruler to draw lines across the circle. This allowed me to add the alphabet, numbers, and my YES/NO marks. I also built my first cardboard pyramid, as I had to "supercharge", my pendulum/pendulum chart for best accuracy.

My interest in pendulums was high again. I was back asking a flood YES/NO, and more complex questions as I could use an alphabet. It was also back to playing games. My cousins had to hide objects for me to use my pendulum to find them. I loved my pendulum. My second attempt at it was successful, but I still enjoyed using it. (Even though I freaked out some of my friends with how accurate I was) I used my pendulum for several years until I turned 13, when I started summer swimming and other activities.

My connection with my pendulum was lost in my teenage years. However, I did regain it in the twenties. Although I was slightly rusty, I didn't lose my dowsing ability. Since then, I've been carrying a pendulum around with me. I started to read pendulum books, bought many pendulums, and even made my own charts as I sought out new ways to use it.

I've used the pendulum to help friends buy reliable used cars, have revealed the sex details of unborn children to people who asked, and have helped people charge mantras with the pendulum for finding love.

Pendulums are used by all walks and professions.

The pendulum allows you to expand your psychic abilities. The best part? Learning to dowse takes very little effort. This brings us to the next chapter: learning how to use the pendulum.

PENDULUM MASTERY

Before you learn how to use your pendulum properly, you must get into the zone. You'll find another central theme to all of my books is "getting into the zone". To achieve the best readings of your pendulum, you must be mentally in the zone. So, let's get started.

Pendulum Accuracy: Getting in the Zone

My books center on the themes of "intention" & "getting into the zone" because it is our intent that unlocks our hidden talents. Your ability to access your hidden talents depends on your intent. Anything you "intend", you can "will" it! You can fuel your intention by being mentally in the zone.

Our cells vibrate continuously, giving off energy signals. Our energy is part of a larger canvas connected to the rest of the universe by an interconnected grid. This is how and to what extent we can dowse infinite possibilities. Our imagination only limits our possibilities.

Although energy is all around us and we are all interconnected, our free will allows us to function as our individual energy system, which happens within our physical bodies. Our free will allows us to decide whether we want our personal energy systems to be clogged, shut down, or to continue functioning normally. This can lead in turn to mental and/or physical illnesses and disease. Free will doesn't come without costs. It is a wonderful gift indeed. But, free will does come with responsibilities. Our lives and our physical health are affected by our choices.

Our bodies have points that allow the flow of higher frequency energy frequencies to our body from this universal grid. This allows us both to energize and to heal physical and mental diseases. These points, also known as chakras, are energy pathways. The meridian is our internal system for spreading the energy throughout our bodies. These systems are more fully covered in The Energy Healing Blueprint.

To start dowsing we need to flush these energy points. Once this is done, you will be able to mentally "in-the zone" and connect to higher consciousness states. You will achieve this by shifting your mental phase so that your conscious and subconscious mind overlap in a way that makes them "in-tune" with the universal consciousness.

Many refer to this as a "hypnagogic" state. But I don't consider it hypnotized because I have altered my mental stage to be more energetically "in tuned" with the universal consciousness.

These steps are the easiest way to get in the zone.

1. Select the area where you intend to dowse. You should not be distracted by television or other noises.

2. Close your eyes. Then, begin to pant. We are going pant to the count 100. Each count will have one inhale followed by one exhale. In other words, you will keep count from 1-100 as, "1(inhale-exhale)---2(inhale-exhale)---100(inhale-exhale)."

3. As you pant, imagine three small balls full of white light. One in the middle of your chest, one under your belly button and one in between your eyes. Imagine each sphere growing in size with each pant. Imagine the spheres colliding and merging together at 20. 40 is the number of spheres that have become one huge ball of light. The light has engulfed your entire body and created a cocoon of light that is almost blinding.

4. Next, picture a bolt white hot lightning coming down from the universe. It would spread out through every vein. You have already seen lightning strike the sky and branch off. Think of the same branching in your own body. However, this white hot energy will never harm or burn you. It

simply cleanses and energizes. Feel the light cleansing every cell. This lightning and sphere o' light are purifying your physical and emotional bodies. This universal lightning bolt flushes your entire body by the 60th birthday.

5. As you continue your panting, notice another copy of you within you. An energy replica is cradled in the stomach. This is your astral form. It should be allowed to grow, fed by the lightning-white sphere until it reaches full size. Then you will feel it pressing down against your skin. Allow it the freedom to penetrate the skin and reach outside of your body in your sphere. Feel the slightly larger body radiate two to three inches off your skin and illuminate a circle around you with the sphere. This should be felt when you reach 80.

6. As you work your way to 100 you can find the silver cord in you that connects to your astral and physical bodies. You can see it. Is it connecting your two bodies from your

crown. From your heart. From your solar system? I won't say "where it connects" as I want you all to decide. Although the cord will be extremely short due to their proximity, it can extend anywhere in the universe where you wish to keep both of them connected. Although this step may seem more relevant to the concepts of my book The Astral Projection Blueprint it is still essential for mental preparation. After you reach 100, you can exhale again and feel the warmth and energy running through you. Do not feel pressure to get to a particular point by the 40th (or 60th) or 80th (or even 20th) pants. It is just important to follow the entire process. However, you should only wear 100 pants.

7. You will be able shift your mental phase to connect your conscious and subconscious minds with the universal consciousness. You should hold a pencil three-four inch from your eyes. At least ten feet from your eyes is a second focal points. It can be a television,

a lit candles, or a digital alarm system readout. First, focus on your pencil until it is in focus. Next, try to focus your eyes on the pencil, allowing it to blur the rest of your vision. Your focus should shift to the pencil. Now, shift your focus slowly back to the television or candle. Your vision will suddenly become otherworldly and the television will appear to be far away. It's almost like you have two focal points in your mind at once. It's almost like the pencil appears magnified. While your secondary focal points become clearer, it will look blurry. Once you achieve this, you will be in the zone.

As you focus on one thing, you might see more pencils than one or two television screens. This is normal. Once you have entered the zone, and locked in between these focal points, the final thing you need to do is see only one of them. This exercise can alter our brain waves to help us see the connections between all things. I am not able to prove this, but it is what my gut instinct tells me.

I feel peaceful and connected to all things when I do the seven steps. I use these seven steps in all of the books I have written to help readers connect with the healing energy of the universe and improve their law of manifestation success.

We are now in the zone. Now let's learn how we can use the pendulum.

Basic Pendulum Dowsing

Now that you are in the zone, it is important to establish a connection between your pendulum and you. You must first teach your pendulum basic questions. Start by tracing a large circle using a piece if paper. Next, trace two lines along the circle's edges. One runs up and down (Northern/South), the other runs sideways (East/West). Add the word YES to the North South line. On the East/West line, write "NO". Next, you will need to suspend your pendulum over the circle. The string, thread, or chains should be held between your thumbs.

It is important that you note that some pendulum manuals will ask you your pendulum if it can show you YES/NO. This means you need to allow your hand to hang and then ask the question aloud: "Show my YES?" Once you have seen the movement (which could either be North-South or East-West), you have established your first base direction of language to indicate YES. If you get a prompt to confirm a No, then repeat the process.

You don't need to ask the Pendulum which direction it is in. It can be programmed to your liking. You can even change the language and swap the directions of your swings.

I asked my pendulum for my YES/NO directions the first time. The YES direction was East-West (East-West), and the NO direction was North-South (North-South). I didn't like these swing directions especially after discovering that the Pendulum Power Board from The National Enquirer had NO and YES reversed to my NO and YES.

What did I do then? My pendulum didn't tell me NO or YES, but I told it. Then I ordered the direction change. I spoke to my Pendulum instinctively with authority. I told it, "This IS YES!" three times per row, as I made my vertical axis swing up and down. Next, I instructed my pendulum with authority three times, telling it "This is NO!" while I made the horizontal axis swing side to side.

Nearly 90% all pendulum users who I've taught get the North - South YES/East-West NO. I've also successfully taught the other 10% how they can change directions but only if the base language was changed. Some 10% prefer to keep their original pendulum base language intact. This allows them to have their YES swing sideways and their NO swing up and back.

If you have an established pendulum language, and would like to keep it in tact. The chart we have prepared for you will tell the pendulum how to swing.

Now it's time for you to program your Pendulum Language. Let's begin with swinging the pendulum North/South along the YES axis. While doing so, say "This IS YES" at least three times. The pendulum should be allowed to swing for at most 20-30 secs. You can mentally repeat the command until your pendulum feels secure.

Next, swing your pendulum sideways (East-West), as you repeat three times "This a NO!" Mentally, continue repeating "This a NO" until it stops swinging. Stop only when your pendulum feels programmed.

Now that we have established the language base for the pendulum we want to ensure that the language is in-tune with your subconscious. You can start by asking a question to which you know an answer. After answering this question, observe your pendulum swing and make sure it moves along the YES North/South axis.

If the pendulum is not swinging along the YES axis, adjust the swing so it follows the YES axis. Next, say it three times loudly, "This IS YES!" Ask the question again, and you will get the correct answer from the pendulum. This will establish a link between you subconscious and your pendulum's appropriate response to all "YES" answers.

Next, ask another question, to which the answer would not be "No", such as the incorrect answer regarding your birthplace. I was born Colorado. So I asked, "Was Georgia my birthplace?" It began to swing right and left along the line that states "NO".

As you might have guessed this will establish the link between the answer for

"NO" and your mind. It's possible to manually move your pendulum in a different direction if it stops swinging in the desired direction. Next, repeat the question with authority.

You might be curious as to what causes the pendulum's swing to shift in the correct direction. It is a result your subconscious directs the nervous system to make small, invisible muscular movements in the hand to shift the swing of pendulum in the proper direction.

In the next few paragraphs, we'll ask you to put this book aside for three full days. This is while you attend 72 hours of "Pendulum Bootcamp Basic Training Bootcamp." The most important thing is to ask simple YES/NO queries. This will give you plenty of time to develop a strong partnership between your pendulum & your subconscious mind.

Your pendulum will improve your accuracy the more you use it. Try to practice your pendulum skills over the next 3 days by asking different YES/NO, TRUE/FALSE and other questions. Questions such as "Will that person call me today?" or "Will the weekend be as planned?". Or you can delve into your history to recall details. There are so many questions you could ask and the limit of what you can ask is your imagination. After three days, you should feel an immediate connection to your pendulum. Then we can go on.

Your pendulum bootcamp does not end there. You will also need to work on your homing or detecting skills. Your pendulum functions as a metal detector and radio antenna. It can also act as a homing device. Your pendulum has a great ability to locate lost objects. You must play "Hide A Key" together with a partner during the three-day period. This game was the same one that I used with my mother. This will improve your ability to tap into "dowsing," the part related to water witching.

The homing capability of a pendulum is the same whether you've lost your keys and are now using it to recall them, or tapping into the universal consciousness to find keys that a friend may have hidden.

You can also have some fun during the three-day training sessions. The Pendulum Cup is a great game to play. One coin should be placed under three red cups. Open your eyes, and you can mix the cups till you lose sight of the coin. Better yet, have a friend play with the cups. Once you have found the right cup, then hold the pendulum up to it and ask the same question. The Pendulum Cup Game is an enjoyable training exercise that will help you improve your dowsing abilities.

No matter what questions are asked during your three days of training, you should always approach each question with childlike anticipation. Instead of thinking yes or no, which can have an impact on the pendulum swings - mentally repeat the question with childlike anticipation. The same principle applies for the games we will play during our three days of training.

Take a three-day rest from this book. Train hard. Ask lots questions and ensure you play both games.

We're glad you are back. We're glad that you made it through the basic training course. Before I go on, I'd like to share some guidance. It is important to start small and unimportant questions when you first begin. Over the past three days you might have become excited and asked some very important questions like "Will I get married in ten year?". However, there are better words. High hopes can also be associated with such an important question. Be aware that your emotions and preconceived feelings about a YES/NO response could impact the outcome.

It is better to ask the simpler and less important questions first. So, for example, if your package is expected to arrive today, ask your pendulum this question: "How many hours until my package arrives today?" Within one hour? Within two hours Within three hours Your pendulum is likely to swing YES. Then wait patiently for your mail to arrive.

I used the phone to check how many calls I.D. received. before I got home. I'd ask, "Do I have one? Two calls? Three calls ?..." to ensure my pendulum swings in my favor.

Note: For anyone who is curious, there is no need to use the chart for YES/NO questions. You can find the answer in midair. I was able to dowse mid-air using only my basic pendulum chart. Once you have the basic language down, you won't need to use a chart. The simple questions can be answered by your pendulum without the need for a chart.

It takes some time to establish a relationship between the pendulum and you before you start exploring more prominent decision-making based off the pendulum's answers. Soon you'll be able to ask whatever question you want.

The outcome of any question, game, or search for lost objects will be affected by your guessing. Do not forget to anticipate the outcome with a child-like spirit. I understand that you might be partial to a specific answer, regardless of whether it is positive or not. However, if you don't remove this thought from your head, you risk changing the outcome or receiving a false one. Your mind should be focused on the actual question. Keep repeating the phrase "I wonder how the answer to my questions will turn out" and you will have great accuracy in dowsing.

We now want to move on to advanced methods of pendulum reading.

Advanced Pendulum Dowsing

You have now successfully passed the three-day translation barrier. Now it's time you can increase your pendulum proficiency. Always remember to "get in the zone" before you start. Also, remember that the antenna extends "you", not the radio receiver. Your antenna will be able to accommodate your wish as long "intending" to receive correct answers.

Before you begin to use the chart below, which was conceptualized based on my recollection of the pendulum board from my childhood, and in cooperation with William Comer from 7dayalchemicalrings, and created by crosssidedesigns.com, there are some basic rules that you must follow to get an accurate reading:

1. Before you start asking questions, make sure to "Get In the Zone". This is key to accurate pendulum readings.

2. Only dowse as you feel. Your readings will not reflect how you feel if your mood is negative, stressed, angry or sad. Emotions can alter the answers.

3. When you ask questions, it is important to remain objective. You can't "hope" for the right answers. Your expectations can affect the outcome of pendulum swings, just as your emotions. Ask each question with child-like expectation. Think about the answer and say it excitedly. It will be as the pendulum connects directly to your subconscious so that it does not influence the answer.

4. Many dowsers will use the "Can? May I? You should answer the three question "Should" before you begin dowsing. Repeat the above three questions three times and check that the pendulum replies with YES or less to each one before you ask a particular question. This could occur when someone asks to see if their spouse has been cheating. This applies to any question, but

most pendulum dowsers believe this only applies to those questions. For example, a friend might ask you to dowse their spouse in order to discover if they are having an affair. This is against the spouse's will. I do not agree that this time is the best time to dowse. However, your intuition as explained in The Extrasensory Perception Blueprint can help you determine whether or not you should.

5. For more difficult questions, beyond the simple "YES/NO", it is worth thinking about how to frame the question so that you get a correct answer. You should consider six factors when asking serious questions: Who is who, when, how much, what, why and where. To give you an example, suppose you are unsure of which college is best for you and are looking for information on the college that offers scholarships. You could ask: "Would Alabama State be in my (whom?) best interest to go to Alabama State (where), where they have a

scholarship (how), Fall Semester (when), to study electronic engineering (why)." This can be repeated for each college that you are interested in attending, until you find the answer.

Although the question you asked is a straightforward YES/NO, it's easy to forget that six points can make it more complicated. So, for example, you might have asked, "Should Alabama State offer me scholarships?" To which you received an affirmative answer. When you pose the same question, asking about two colleges that offer scholarships, you also get a yes. This is because your subconscious already knows you should attend college. You didn't choose which college you would prefer to attend. So, your subconscious knows that you should attend college. The colleges all have YES answers.

We now know how to create 6-point questions. Let's take a closer look at this Master Pendulum Chart:

As you can clearly see, the Master Pendulum Chart contains many details. You will find the usual YES/NO, alphabet, 0-9 digits, days of each week, months in the year, signs of the horoscope, and other markings that are drawn in the corners of an outer circle of Master Pendulum Chart.

This Master Pendulum Chart was specially created to make dowsing more accurate. To open your eBook, simply take a picture to save it as a photo on your smartphone. Once you have signed up to my mailing lists, you will be able to download the full resolution chart.

If you don't have the necessary markings, you can make small cardboard pyramids and place them in the middle of the Master Pendulum Chart. A pendulum reading can be requested by friends. We'll be covering all of these points soon.

Get out your pendulum and spend a while experimenting with Master Pendulum charts. You'll be surprised at what you discover when you take a look at the choices on this chart. If you are satisfied with the information, then go ahead and look at the broken down of each chart.

YES/AM & Man-This line connects the Yang/masculine energies and the aethers. It can be used by the Sun to recharge and revitalize living organisms, including animals, plants, and minerals. It is used in order to receive your YES answer. This can be combined with the 0-9 time chart times to specify the time of day. For example, 3:00 p.m. This line is also used to indicate the unspecified sexual partner of a baby-boy.

NO/PM/Woman: This line connects to Yin/feminine energies found in the Aethers. It can also be used to send energy from the Moon to any living thing (plant, animal, mineral) for calming, rebalancing, and/or restoring balance. It can be used in order to receive your NO responses. It can also be used with the 0-9 numerical chart times to specify the morning's time, such a 3:00AM. This line can also used to indicate the unknown sex of baby girls. Let's talk about each symbol of the inner quadrants.

The Four Symbols -There also are four symbols within each quadrant of a pendulum circle that make up a tetragrammaton. These letters, or "Yod Hey Viv Hey," are the four letters in the tetragrammaton. This charge charges the Master Pendulum Chart. You can use this to increase your intuition to find accurate answers and manifest your desires. Let's now break down each letter of tetragrammaton.

Lower Left Quadrant - This symbol is located in the lower corner of a central circle. It's the first letter from the Tetragrammaton. "Yod" represents masculine energy.

Upper Left Quadrant-The symbol located in the upper corner of a central circle is the second Tetragrammaton letter, "Hey". This symbol represents feminine energy.

Lower Right Quadrant-The symbol found in the lower corner of central circle's upper right is the third Tetragrammaton Letter, "Vov." The symbol represents masculine energy.

Upper Right Quadrant-The symbol found in the upper corner of a central circle's center circle is the fourth Letter of Tetragrammaton (pronounced "Hey") This represents feminine energies and the element Earth.

Numbers/Alphabet. The Master Pendulum Chart's inner circle contains the first and last rings. These represent letters and numbers. The numbers 0-9 may be used to answer many questions. You can use the alphabet in a very similar way to the Ouija Board. But, we are not talking to spirits. We communicate with our subconscious mind and the universal consciousness in order to relay complex messages.

When using the number and alphabet charts, ensure your answers are correct. Hold your pendulum at the center of the chart while you ask your question. Once your answer is given, state your thoughts aloud. Write down any number or letter on a piece if the pendulum swings toward a number. The pendulum may then move on to the next number/letter without hesitation, as it knows that you have received the correct answer.

If you are having trouble finding your cell phones after you have searched your house, car, and home looking for them, and your pendulum doesn't move, it is time to get out your chart. Now, look at the last time you were able to see your phone, and ask where it was. To ask the question "Can someone please tell me where (where), I (who), lost (why) my cell phone this morning (when), so we can retrieve (how).

As your pendulum begins to swing, hold it high above your chart. Speak aloud to the pendulum and begin writing down the words.

I-N-L-U-K-E-S-G-A-R-A-G-E

You suddenly remembered dropping your nephew Jason off at your brother's place. Jason had spent the evening with Mark, his son, and was now ready for the baseball match. You saw your brother at his garage and jumped out of the car to say hello. Luke was getting ready to cut your grass. After the lawn mower didn't start, you remember sitting down at Luke's desk and giving Luke a hand. Before you left, it was gone.

Pendulums are not magical. The point is, that most questions, such as "Where did you leave your cell phone?" are subconsciously answered. The memory is only hidden or submerged and should be brought to light.

Note: When you're dealing with situations like this, where you lose your keys and a cell phone or other personal items, I understand the urgency and can help you to think of six points. Relax, your pendulum is still functional. A simple question like "Where is the cell phone?" would yield the same result. To help you remember it, I only added the six point question. I will not repeat the six points process for the remainder. Six-point questions can be better served when they are very serious. For example, deciding whether it is in the best interests of you to move to Hawaii for a job. Yes, the beach sounds fantastic, but is it in your best interest to make the move? Here is where you should use the six point question technique.

Let me jump ahead to explain the outer circle's second ring. Now let us discuss the numbering-ring ring. The number chart is a tool that can be used to help us understand how. There are many ways. You can pose the following questions: "On an order of 1 to 10," with the 0 marking 10. You can use numbers to find a phone number and/or address. The numbers can be used to identify the time and date. You can also use this numbering chart to dowse specific frequencies. This is an advanced method that deals with radionics. Radionics is based in the fact everything vibrates at certain frequencies.

Here are some other examples.

1. 1-10 scale - Before using the number table to ask "On an order of 1-10 questions", you should first repeat three times: "When I ask the next (or any) question(s), "0 equals 10, before proceeding. It's possible to then ask a precise question like "On an 1-10 scale, how much will I like the new Chinese restaurant where we will be dining tonight?"

2. Phone numbers, addresses-If you have lost your phone number or forgotten its

number, you may use the number table to locate it. To find an exact address you have lost, you can use a number chart that is prior to the alphabet.

3. Healing Frequencies-If radionics is your preferred method of healing, the chart can be used to first determine the frequency at which a blockage occurs, such as the frequency you experience with your current migraine. To dislodge the blockage, make a number that would equal 10 for each number in the migraine frequency. For example, you could use a piece 23697 to address an 87413 frequency illness. You can then write a number that would make each individual migraine frequency equal 10 to have a healing session.

4. Time of the day/night - You can also use our numbering system to find the time. For instance, "When does Jenny get home?" If Jenny's pendulum swings to 1, 0, 1, 1 and 8, it will be 10:18. To further explain the time of day or night, ask "Is that 10:18 AM? or

PM?". The pendulum will swing sideways if it is 10:18 pm.

Days of The Week/Months on the Year-Rings Three and Four represent the days of each week and month. The days of a week can be used to get answers that are specific to a given day. You can find answers to questions related to months of year using the months section of the year. This can be used together with the numbering graph. For example, you could ask your son, "At how much on which hour of the month will my boy return home from his trip in Europe?" To get an answer like, "7:30 am, Monday, August 8.

I've heard of dowsers using the chart for determining the age artifacts they have discovered. One dowser found an old bullet and was able to establish that it belonged in the Civil War era by asking about its age. The bullet was then authenticated using a Historian.

Horoscope: The Horoscope can help answer any questions you may have about the zodiac sign. I am not an expert on astrology but I'm sure that others who are are more familiar with the subject can find other ways to use this chart.

Master Pendulum Chart has many uses. As you gain proficiency with the chart and use it frequently, you might place an orgonite (or crystal) or cardboard pyramid inside the circle. You align each flat edge along a line, each corner resting on one of the letters in the tetragrammaton. This will make your pendulum chart more powerful and clean. In The Pyramid Energy Blueprint, you will learn how to make pyramids.

Here you have it. A concise Master Pendulum Diagram to answer most of the questions. Some situations may require the chart to be updated. If you need to know which gemstones are best for energized meditation rooms, then this chart is the one you should use. It would be wonderful to have a chart listing between 30-50 of the most popular gemstones. A chart with 30-50 gemstones may be useful if you are looking for the best herb to help you sleep. Only if your pendulum chart listed several dozen herbs!

Making your own charts is the best way to go in either case. Simply draw a circle. Next, add all possible names for any gemstones or herb you may consider using to the outside of the circle. Next, draw lines from each name of a herb or gemstone to the center. To choose the best remedy for your problem, you can hold your pendulum near the center of a chart.

The Master Pendulum Chart still has its place. It can help you identify THE best gem or herb, so don't overlook this incredible chart. If you'd like to see a larger version the Master Pendulum Chart you can get it in jpeg or as png from Author's Blueprint Community Page. The link is at the end. As well, you can order a Master Pendulum

Board from 7dayalchemicalrings.co. William Comer custom makes Master Pendulum Boards upon request. Let's look at some advanced applications of the pendulum.

ADVANCED PEENDULUM APPLICATIONS

We've discussed how to use your pendulum to ask YES/NO and how the Master Pendulum Chart works. Finally, we covered how to apendulum as a navigation device for finding objects like oil, water or lost cell phones. While we know a lot about how to use the pendulum in general, there is so much more. Here are some advanced techniques.

The Clockwise, Counterclockwise Swing

Before I can proceed, let me first introduce two additional pendulum movement to your pendulum system. They are the clockwise or counterclockwise swing. These movements are vital for advanced pendulum applications. Let's start by programming each new swing in our pendulum languages.

Begin by swinging your pendulum clockwise. Then, command aloud three time: "This will send positive energy!" After that, allow the pendulum's swing to continue for at least 30 second or longer. Next, counterclockwise swing your pendulum and repeat the command three times. "This is removing negativity!" Allow the pendulum's swing to continue for at least 30 second or more, until you feel the connection.

Pendulums can be used for positive energy transmission or removal of stagnant/negative energy. They are crucial for healers, dowsers, and others who wish to use Master Pendulum Charts for healing and/or manifestation.

Pendulum Healing (Self Healing)

A pendulum can be used for healing. You can use both the clockwise as well as counterclockwise swings. This is a very simple process if you're working on self healing. It is possible to imagine yourself receiving an overwhelming flow of healing energy pulling from every direction. Begin to turn the pendulum counterclockwise. Consider the positive healing energies being drawn into your auric fields from the Earth below you and the sky. Your pendulum may swing wildly for a while until it finally calms down and settles. Once the pendulum stops, you are "filled up to the brim" with healing energy and fully charged.

It is possible that you are suffering from an illness such as a terrible sinus infection. If this is your case, turn your pendulum counterclockwise and think of your sinus infections as a magnet. Allow the pendulum "pull out the infection" and gather the negative energy from the sinus infection. It can swing wildly for a few minutes before it stops. Keep in mind that negative energy is transmuted instantly into the aethers, rendering it harmless until it is balanced back into a universal energy field.

Now, the pendulum should start to move clockwise in order to send healing energy to your body. As the pendulum swings, your sinuses can be seen. Let it swing till it stops.

You may be wondering how I know the negative energy has been transformed back into the realm of the aethers. This transmutation happens because truth is what you see when you read my intention. This truth is my intention. You don't need to be concerned about stagnant energy gathering around you. Download the Master Blueprint Sigil and you can further strengthen this intention once you've joined Author's's's's's's's's's's's's's's' Community Blueprint Page.

Pendulum Healing (Healing Others)

You can use the same process to heal yourself and then work with someone else.

A picture of the person you wish to heal can be placed in the center your Master Pendulum Chart. Universal healing energies don't need to be located far away and can work from anywhere. Next, raise your hand above the picture, and repeat the statement three times.

The pendulum should begin to swing over the photo. If the person requires negative or stagnant energy to be removed, the Pendulum will first swing counterclockwise. This creates an atmosphere that will "suck" any negative energy out the person. It will then release it harmlessly through aethers and out into space where it can be balanced. Once the pendulum has stopped swinging, it will stop swinging and go clockwise to send healing power into the person.

This process can take a few minutes, or even an hours depending on what is needed.

Once you are an expert pendulum healer, you will be able to use the power and intent to speed this up by directing the entire healing session within 10 minutes. Just repeat the following three times: "I command for this healing session to be completed in ten minutes." Now you will only need to say it three more times.

The healing session will still be potent, even if the sessions last only 10 minutes. You've just increased the speed at the which the energies were removed and received. This is optional. If your intuition says to slow down when you're dealing with someone in pain, go slower.

There are many different ways to use the pendulum in healing. These are just a few of the options that are listed in The Energy Healing Blueprint.

Pendulum healing work should not be done without a copper or brass pendulum. Your pendulum will not retain the energy pattern or "imprint" from the illness. Your pendulum may not be able to take on the vibration of the illness, even though the negative energies have been dispersed into aethers. This can be avoided by using a brass or a copper pendulum.

If you are using a pendulum made from brass or copper (e.g. John the Conqueror root) I HIGHLY recommend that you hang it in a small pyramid. To clean out vibrational patterns, allow your pendulum's to swing freely from the pyramid's apex for a few hours. Don't be alarmed that your pendulum is swinging completely by itself. There are powerful energies associated with pyramid structures. The Pyramid Energy Blueprint can help you make your own pyramid.

Pendulum Manifestation Techniques

The Law of Manifestation Blueprint contains most of my manifestation strategies, but this particular technique is better described here. To manifest a specific action, like a raise or a raise in pay, write a six-point directive on a piece of newspaper. Then place it at the center of The Law of Manifestation Blueprint. Next, place your pendulum above the written instruction and then read it aloud three more times. Then repeat the process clockwise as your mind repeats the words. Repeat the command mental until the pendulum stops swimming. You have now submitted the formal request.

Let's say you've been doing the same job ten years. Even though you handle two other worker assignments, you haven't received a pay rise in more than four decades. You can hand-write to receive the raise.

"I (whom), formally request that my boss (how), grant me an appropriate pay rise (what), at my job(where) by the end-of July (when), because it is something I truly deserve (why).

The Law of Manifestation Blueprint explains how to proceed. You can also stick your handwritten letter in your purse or wallet so you can carry it around until it is made public. The above request could be written better, but I believe you get the point. The six-point process is what we follow. You don't have to worry if you don't get the raise. The request was made. I promise you that the universe is going to send you what is in your best interests. Be patient.

Subconscious Pendulum Programming

Subconscious Pendulum Programme is a way for your mind to be programmed. You use a pendulum and remove negative thoughts patterns to make room for positive thoughts. The subconscious mind responds to all stimuli. One source that is often neglected is emotion. Your subconscious links all of your past experiences with emotions. Take a look at a painful experience. Relive that painful memory. Are you upset that such an event is still a part of your past? Imagine a time when you were happy. Do you find it brings a smile?

Memories that are filled with strong emotions will often remain in your main memories for years. Emotional experiences can make you the person that you are today. Negative emotional connections can spread like viruses to your mind.

I have a hate relationship with fish. My childhood experience with Long John Silvers fish caused food poisoning. I clearly remember being violently ill. I was so upset when it ended that I was unable to go outside to play with Ronnie. The memory of that incident kept me from ever eating Long John Silvers again for twenty years. I think my subconscious connected food poisoning to fish. This thought had the effect of a virus, affecting my reactions to fish. This association was not broken until I applied the subconscious pendulum programming method.

Your pendulum can help you to erase your mental "virus" and attachments to painful emotions or negative thoughts. You need to end the negative cycle, if you are constantly telling yourself that you're a failure. This is done using the pendulum. Start by swinging the pendulum counterclockwise. After that, repeat the words aloud three times: "I'm A Failure." Continue to allow the pendulum twirl on its own, until it stops.

As you will recall, a counterclockwise movement is a "removing" motion. It helps to erase negative thoughts and memories. It will grasp the negative vibrations and "draw them out" of you, much like a magnet.

Allow the pendulum clockwise to continue swinging until it slows to a complete halt. When I was done, I mentally repeated my words "I hate Long John Silvers fish", three more times.

Once the pendulum stops completely, you can reprogram your subconscious to have a positive belief replace the one you just released. Now that you have cleared your mind of the "I feel like a failure", thought, you must insert into your subconscious the positive alternative to the negative thought. This would be "I am successful," three times per row. Next, start swinging your ndulum clockwise. Keep repeating the phrase mentally as the pendulum moves. Keep going until your pendulum stops swinging. This could take as little as 30 seconds or as long at twenty minutes.

Once the pendulum stops swinging, it means that you have successfully reprogrammed yourself. In my instance, I said three times out loud, "I love Long John Silvers fish". After the pendulum started to swing clockwise, I allowed it it to continue spinning as I mentally repeated this statement to my mind, until it stopped.

This simple method can be used to move towards a positive, productive mindset and to let go of any doubts or negative thought patterns. There are other methods that can be used with this method. They are listed in The Manifestation Blueprint (and The

Energy Healing Blueprint), but these are the ones that are most appropriate.

This method works in any way. It is important to remember that the pendulum should swing counterclockwise when you want to remove negative thought patterns. Your thoughts will be positively charged if the pendulum is moving clockwise. Allow the pendulum its natural pace. It might swing very fast and wild or it might keep a moderate, even faster pace. Allow the pendulum continue to swing until it stops moving on its own.

Now it's time for you to take control. You can now think about one negative thought and use the subconscious program pendulum technique.

Body Dowsing

If you are in a situation where your pendulum is needed but don't have it, or you're worried about people thinking you're crazy, you can use you body as a guide.

Simply move your body back and forward while saying three times "This is YES!" Continue to sway to the point where you feel the connection. Next, continue to sway side to side while you repeat aloud "This is NO!" Your body will now use the same language to communicate with your pendulum.

Now, let's check the body pendulum. Next time that you're fruit picking in the grocery stores, pick the ripest fruit you can see and hold it at solar plexus. Mentally ask "Is this ripest plum I can purchase?" If you don't sway from side to side, you should search for fresher fruit.

You can also test it with several different brands of vitamins. If you need chewable Vitamin C and there are three brands available, you could pick up one of each and place it near your solar panel. You would then ask the brand you prefer to be the best.

This technique can also be used to find out if a particular food, vitamin or herb is right for you. Hold it in front of your solar plexus. Do not ask questions. Then, note the direction your body begins moving. If it sways from one side to the other, you can choose the best vitamin, herb or food for your needs.

These suggestions will work for body-pendulum dowsing as well as regular pendulum use.

The Finger-Click Approach

The finger-click technique is a faster and easier way to say YES/NO. Make a circle with your thumb (right hand if you are right-handed, left hand if you are left-handed) and stick your pointer fingers in the middle. To break the circle, move you pointer finger. Keep your pointer finger out to break the circle. Repeat this three more times.

After you've said NO, you can go through the same process to give your YES. Keep your pointer fingers from striking the circles with your pointer fingers. You can repeat this process three times.

You now have your fingers programmed to answer YES- and NO-question. The finger method works just like the bodypendulum method but is more discreet.

Pendulum secrets you didn't know

The pendulum makes it a great tool for diagnosing or receiving information. This is its most widespread use. You might not know that this is also a powerful tool for creating energy fields. This will help you attract what you want.

This groundbreaking book will show how to:

* Avoid negative energy-producing people and places

* Energize any person, place, object or thing with any frequency

* Send energy at any frequency to anyone, any place or thing

* Speed up healing

* Protect anyone using protective energy

* Rapidly accelerate the materialization your desires

The Best Type of Pendulum

When choosing a pendulum, there are two options. You can buy one already made or make one. Premade pendulums are often preferred by people who like the look of premade tools. Home-made pendulums can be used for comfort because they are imbued in their own energy.

It is important to choose the option you feel most connected with. This will allow you to eliminate negative feelings, increase your pendulum power, and remove any negativity.

Why Pendulum Magic Works

The principle of manipulating the energy fields is what makes pendulum magic work. The vortex created by your intention and the spinning the pendulum acts as a magnet that attracts what you want.

You can also utilize the energy field-creation ability of the pendulum for any effect, from weather manipulation to healing other people to increasing your personal wealth.

This book will show you how create manifesting energy field and disperse bad energy fields.

The Primary Pendulum Movements

Your pendulum's movement will be in three primary directions

Clockwise - For creating energy fields and filling space, objects, with energy.

Counterclockwise: To remove unwelcome energies

Side to side: For neutralizing unwanted energies.

You might discover that your pendulum moves in opposite directions. It's okay.

Cleansing Your Pendulum

You must clean your pendulum to ensure you create powerful fields of manifestation intention. You don't want to start your work with a dirty pendulum. The cleansing process can be described as follows:

1. Place your left palm over your pendulum.

2. Then, in this position, declare to yourself: "I remove all the negative energy from my pendulum." Repeat this intention at minimum three times. This is the most important step in achieving an internal understanding of the concept.

3. Any negative energy lodged in your pendulum will be taken and recycled in the following ways:

You can raise your right arm to the sky, and then state to yourself: I send this energy from source to make it love and light.

You should then be freed from any negative energy. You can continue the cleaning and recycling process as many as you like. You can also cleanse your pendulum by placing it into a bowl of salt for three days. Combining these methods will ensure your manifesting tools are super-clean.

If your pendulum is found to be clear, you can give it positive energy.

Charging Your Pendulum

Your pendulum works as a manifesting tool. Every tool needs a source of power. How to charge your pendulum with the energy and power of the creator in order to allow it to manifest your dreams. Here's what you need to do:

1. Get creative energy flowing by lifting your hands up towards the sky, with your palms facing upwards.

2. Now you can say to God, "Divine Father in Heaven, fill me" several times. After a few minutes, you will start to feel sensations throughout your hands, especially your palms. This is the Heavenly Dad's creative heavenly energy. Take a deep breath and allow this energy to flow through you for as long time as it pleases.

3. Once you're done basking the glow of God, take your pendulum in your right-hand and state:

"I fill your heart with the love and light from the creator of heavens and earth." Do this repeatedly. The pendulum will start to charge and you'll feel the power you just got.

Now your pendulum will help you to realize your dreams.

Tuning Your Pendulum To You

This is a simple and important step that ensures your pendulum's operation. It's just like making sure your keys are correct for your car. Your car won't work if you have the wrong keys.

Tuning your pendulum enables you to connect it with your unique energy field, so that every part of your spirit can use it. It can also give you information about your entire being. It takes only a few steps. Here's the way:

1. You can hold your pendulum with the string between your right and left palms.

2. After about a minute, it will start to turn in a particular direction depending on how strong your energy polarity is. Allow the pendulum to spin for about a minute.

3. You now have your pendulum tuned to you and are ready to use it in manifesting.

Clearing Out Objects Using Your Pendulum

It is easy to clear items of negative energies with your pendulum. This can be used to remove negative energy from objects like jewelry or pain points. This process disperses negative energy by unwinding your negative energy field. The process is as follows

1. Place the object in question on a flat surface.

2. Move your pendulum to the object and repeat the following command.

"Clear this object (name) of negative energie."

3. At this point, it should begin to rotate counterclockwise. This is the sign that the pendulum was beginning to deflect the negative energy field emanating from the object.

4. Let the pendulum continue spinning until it stops.

If the pendulum stops then the process of unwinding negative energy has begun. If you feel that it is necessary, you may repeat the entire process.

This process can be used as a way to get rid of negative energies from food. You can also use it for clearing away negative energy that is physically present. To remove negative energy,

1. Stand at the location you suspect is a source of negative energy.

2. You can stand there while you hold your pendulum.

"Clear out this negative energy space."

3. Allow the pendulums to spin for as much time as you are able.

4. If the pendulum stops, then the cleansing process is completed or has begun.

5. This process can be repeated as many times you want.

To remotely cleanse a space, you will need a witness. You may need a photograph, a fragment of the structure, and even the name of your location on a piece or paper. Once you have the witness, go ahead and do the following:

1. Place your pendulum on the witness.

2. The pendulum can be used to dispel negative energy.

3. Allow the pendulum spinning to continue for a minute or less.

4. The cleansing process begins when the pendulum stops.

5. Repeat the clearing process until you are satisfied.

Once you've cleared the target, send that negative energy back to Source.

1. Move your pendulum across the space that you have cleared.

2. Ask the Divine Designer to transform negative energy in love and light.

3. The pendulum should spin in the desired direction for at minimum one minute before your arm gets tired.

4. When the pendulum stops the transmutation process is over.

This is an amazing process that you can use when you feel fearful or sad. Transmute your negative emotions to universal love and infinite brightness. You can even transform negative energies in a distant location by this process and a witness.

Charging objects using your pendulum

By commanding your pendulum to charge an object, your pendulum reverses the energy dispersal process. This technique allows you to imbue objects and other objects with positive energy. Positives that are charged with positive energy can be used to create talismans which radiate good luck into the environment. This can be used as a way to fill wounds or cut that have had negative energy removed.

Here's what you can do:

1. Clear negative energy by using the techniques discussed in the chapter.

2. Place your pendulum on the object and command it with positive energy. This energy can be anything you feel is positive. It could be love or light, happiness, joy, and so forth. I have had incredible results with objects charged with the energy of belly laughing!

3. Allow the pendulum and your arm to spin until they stop, or until you get tired.

4. Once you're done charging the object, make sure your pendulum seals it in. Allow the pendulum's spin to continue for as long time as you like. The pendulum will stop spinning once it reaches a halt.

5. Repeat the process as many times you feel it is necessary.

Sending energy and support to others

With the help your pendulum, it is possible to easily send energy any where you like. You can either meet the person face-to-face, or remotely. For the second process to work, you will need a witness.

For a better understanding of how the process works, try thinking in terms of sending a specific vibration.

This is how you can fill an individual with a particular energetic pattern when you're sharing the same space:

1. Allow the person to sit comfortably. They can also lie on their backs.

2. The crown chakra is your focus.

3. Tell your pendulum that you want to send the right energy frequency to the person in

front. Allow the pendulum and its spin to continue as long as it feels good.

4. To seal the energy within the person, ask the pendulum to stop. Let the pendulum continue to move as long you feel it is right.

5. The process can be repeated as many times you feel it is necessary.

Increase Your Energy Fields' Power

By holding a crystal with your left hand, you can greatly increase the power of your energies generated by your pendulum. A crystal can be held in your left hand. Energy enters your body through the left side and is projected through the right.

The crystal you choose should be related to the desired outcome. For example, a quartz stone in your left hand would increase the vortex's strength, while a citrine will draw money, carnelian for vitality and health, and sunstone would provide protection and healing. There are many options.

You can also use items that have the desired frequency to create energy fields. Take, for instance, the frequency of a waterfall. You can project this energy into the vortex using your left hand.

Making A Manifesting Titan

This technique will allow you to create powerful talismans which manifest power using your pendulum. Then, follow the following steps:

1. Choose a piece that is clean. These talismans are best created on unlined papers. You will also need a pencil, and a pendulum.

2. The sheet of paper should contain all your wishes. Use all of your senses and describe the desired condition as accurately as you can.

3. After you're done folding the piece of paper, place your pendulum onto it.

4. For your desire to be fulfilled, you can command the pendulum to turn on. To flood it with love & light Your pendulum will spin as long and as it pleases.

5. When you're done with your work, keep the sheet in your bag, wallet, or some other safe place. You can also keep it under your pillows at night.

6. This talisman can be energized at minimum twice daily

This kind of manifestation magic can have unlimited possibilities. You can create and energize protection, love drawing talismans full of power, and success-drawing magical talismans.

Using the Power Of The Moon and Sun

Now that your dream manifesting tool is convenient and powerful, you should take advantage of the most powerful manifestation device in nature: the moon.

The moon is a great source of power you can redirect into your thoughts. The moon's phases can be used to empower you by riding the wave.

The waning of the moon is the most effective time to eliminate negative energy and remove things from your life.

The best time for you to draw is during the waxing moon. This is when the moon expands in size.

The creator gave us another powerful source to our energy: the sun. By creating your talismans or thoughtforms during the hours leading to noon, you can increase your thoughtforms' power. The sun rises to its highest point, so too does its power.

If you face the sun or moon with your left hand, you can harness the power of these celestial bodies. Inhale the power at minimum 3 times, maximum 9 times to build a charge. Next, use your pendulum and proceed to manifest.

What is the Pendulum?

History of the Pendulum

Pendulums can be described as a weight attached or chained to a string. A pendulum may be as simple as an attached washer to a piece a string, or as complex as one can imagine.

For casual observers, pendulum use is easy: Pick up the unweighted end or chain and ask a few questions. The pendulum will then swing. It isn't that easy though. This guide will give you all the information you need to be a skilled dowser in no matter how much time.

Dowsing allows people to find hidden objects and receive information. They use some kind of dowsing instrument to observe their responses to a series or questions. This ancient practice often uses pendulums. In fact, the Cairo Museum boasts pendulums that date back to over 1,000 years. Dowsing still exists today.

It's used to find water and precious metals. According to the American and British societies for dowsers, it can also be used underground to find features such as caves and tunnels. Oil, veins of minerals or underground building services are all possible uses of dowsing. Even missing people or pets can be found.

Pendulum dowsing offers more benefits than mere material objects. This powerful tool can help you find answers to questions regarding your past, present, or future.

What is the Pendulum Really Doing?

Once it was believed that supernatural forces like angels or demons were responsible for the movement. Today we know that motion is caused primarily by "ideomotor reaction" which is a small movement of your hand that receives its instructions via your subconscious brain. Our subconscious mind responds to questions by stimulating the nerve endings within our fingers. This causes the pendulum in response to our question to swing. Our body outwardly reveals our inner knowing.

Even though we are aware that the pendulum swings because your hand responds to your brain's commands, we still haven't figured out how the subconscious processes the information to determine which way the pendulum will move.

If we already know the answer, it is easy for the pendulum to respond to our question.

Some believe that the subconscious mind determines how the brain will move the mineral or water dowsing device in cases like water and mineral dowsing.

Others believe that the subconscious mind acts to open the door to what Carl Jung called the "collective conscious." In either case, the subconscious may have access to a universal library of information.

There are no hard and fast answers. So we evaluate the effectiveness, usefulness, and efficacy of divination using our personal experience.

Be ready to plunge into the magic and wonder of the pendulum!

Pendulum buying or making

After understanding what makes the pendulum move we can now find, make, or purchase something to use as a peduncle.

Pendulums are very easy to create and use. The pendulum can be attached to any string or chain and has enough weight to hold it down. Pendulums are portable, so you can keep them with you wherever your travels take you.

Making a Pendulum

To make a simple pendulum, tie a length of string to the end of a washer. The pendulum will move more easily if the string is too long. Start with a length of seven inches.

You'll determine what length works best for your needs -- some prefer a length just 4 inches.

Here are some other items you could use for a pendulum.

* A chain necklace that contains a medallion locket or charm

* A key tied to string or twine

* A string teemed with a heavy beads

* A fishing weigh tied to a length of fishing line

* A stone encased in string

* A ring suspended by a piece o string or thread

You can also suspend your pendulum by attaching a medium-sized piece of bead to the end string. Tie a large knot to the string at the top if you don't already have a pendulum. You will have something to hold onto during dowsing sessions. Pendulums can be made from many different materials by visiting your local arts-and-crafts store. You may be able to create some stunning pendulums by using some simple jewelry-making skills, if not you're very handy.

When making your pendulum, listen to your instincts. It must be in tune with your energy. You might find that a piece made of petrifiedwood suits you the best.

Buying a Pendulum

Pendulums can also be purchased online at metaphysical and new age shops. The majority are made with semiprecious stones, such as aventurine or amethyst. Others are made with metals - the most common are copper, silver, brass.

People use different pendulums for different types and questions. So, once you are comfortable with basic pendulum reading, you might be interested in exploring which pendulum will best answer the question. People like rose quartz and carnelian when they have questions about love. The protective energy of black crystals is strong, and many people use pendulums with blue colors to answer health questions. Ask the pendulum whether it is the best one for your specific question.

The best way to get your first pendulum is to go in person. Buy the pendulum from the shop. While the pendulum will not be tuned to your specific energy, it can give you an indication of your intuition. How does your energy interact with the pendulum?

It's easy to experiment with these methods using a simple pendulum. You can start by making a simple design, like the washer and strings model or a jewelry.

It is also helpful to keep a book or journal handy to note the information you receive during your pendulum session.

A Pendulum for Every Purpose

Yay! Congratulations! As you know, choosing a pendulum to resonate with your energy is key.

Pendulums are made of specific materials to serve specific purposes. For advanced pendulum work, you should choose the one that is most appropriate for your primary purpose. That's why it is good to have a variety of them. Be clear about the goals that you have for your pendulum, and consider which materials will be most beneficial to your work.

You can even have different shapes! For more information on how to choose the right pendulum, read this article!

Shapes

Circle (ball), - This ancient and universal symbol stands for unity, wholeness, infinite, the goddess, and female strength. The circle symbolises the sacred and the spiritual, along with the "sacred", Earth. This is a wonderful shape that can be used for many purposes, especially for women.

Diamond (faceted). -- Because it is perfectly symmetrical, the diamond vibrates towards harmony. It's a good shape for asking questions about your family, home, hearth, and friends.

Heart -- Hearts symbolize love. Therefore, this shape is ideal for people who are looking to find true love, happiness and lasting love.

Octagon -- A symbol representing the "best" portion of psychic substance. It is also the vehicle for spiritual light. The octagon symbolises the nearness to heaven that the psychic elements possess, which is why it is an ideal shape for working with angels and spirits.

Star -- Also known under the merkaba name, it's a sign of love, joy, prosperity, protection from fires, good luck, hope and love. The merkaba, a divine light vessel that is said to have been used by ascended masters in order to connect with people from the higher realms, is the reputed use of the merkaba. This pendulum can be used to contact spirits, and it is particularly effective for spirit guides.

Colors

These are the traditional names for crystals (metals and wood), as well the colors used in pendulums.

This is a good guideline for choosing the color of a pendulum. Your pendulum will be more effective if it is the correct color for the subject you are trying to reach.

Red Pendulum -- Use it to ground emotions, passions and charisma.

Orange Pendulum - Represents sexual fire and abundance in career, projects, or for anything that needs an extra "push."

Yellow Pendulum -- The colour of power, love and devotion to man and the sun. It also represents connection to your higher power.

Green Pendulum -- Success in life, fertility, growth, success with ideas and things that increase our sense of hope.

Blue Pendulum: Protection, peace, tranquility and spirituality

Indigo Pendulums: Richness of meditation and twilight. Deep emotions. Seriousness and contemplation.

Violet Pendulums: Use this color for connection with the highest Universal power along with the sacred.

White Pendulums: Bring in the power the moon to allow energy to flow easily

Black Pendulums -- Provide protection, so use in cases

Multicolor Pendulum -- Represents all rainbow colors and is closely related to Chakra centers. This pendulum is ideal if you're looking for information about blocked, imbalanced, or balanced Chakras.

Materials

Clear Quartz -- You already know that quartz is an excellent energy amplifier. This material is very clear and clear. It boosts energy and creates clear energy flows.

This pendulum is an excellent choice for communicating with spirits or Spirit Guides.

Amethyst/Chakra Stones -- Amethyst will open your third eyes. The pendulum can be used to reach a steady, calm place of centeredness.

This pendulum can help you to amplify healing energies, eliminate negative energy and create balance. It is great for clearing out negative energy and asking health questions.

Aventurine -- Attracts abundance and promotes healing. It also clears and protects one's heart chakra. This makes it ideal for emotional release. Fears are released and the heart is open to new possibilities.

This pendulum can be used for all matters of the heart, from questions about friends and family to emotional healing.

Onyx - A strong protective stone which absorbs and transforms any negative energy.

This is a wonderful pendulum to use if your concern is about worry or anxiety.

Brass -- Attracts health, wealth and protection. It is associated the element of Fire and is extremely energizing.

You can also use a brass pendulum to heal financial and other questions. The fire energy can help you solve any problem.

Copper -- Can be used to amplify any type od energy instead of clear quartz

Silver -- This silver is another powerful energy amplifier that can be used in lieu of clear quartz, copper, or both.

Wood -- Wood pendulums may be beautiful but are not efficient energy conductors. Choose a heavy wood pendulum so it doesn't blow around in the breeze. However, it shouldn't be too heavy to swing.

Cage pendulums -- Cage pendulums often contain silver which is a powerful energy amplifier. To increase the power of your pendulum working, you can insert some meaning into it. For example, herbs or clear quartz chips. Use your intuition when adding items to your pendulum-session.

Alright! You're now on your way towards becoming a pendulum expert. Learn all about the following:

* Mental preparation

* How you can hold your pendulum

* There are two methods to program your pendulum

* Caring for your pendulum

* How you phrase questions to get the most precise responses

Get Started With Your Pendulum

Mental Preparation

Although the preparation for using your pendulum isn't difficult, it is vital to clearly state your intentions. These steps can be used for basic dowsing. We'll discuss more sophisticated and specialized uses of a pendulum in a later article. A sacred place is one that you can find. This could be your kitchen, or out in the forest, or at an alter -- whatever place you find spiritually interesting and comforting.

It doesn't matter how much you focus, but it is essential that you don't get interrupted. Practice daily, if you can. Once you have mastered the use of the pendulum, it is possible to do this silently from anywhere. It doesn't matter if you're working, it just takes a moment to find a private place or wait for the quieter moments. You can do this even from your car!

* Clear your mind. No preconceived notions or expectations of what's going to happen. No expectations, no ego, no desired outcomes.

* Hold your pendulum. You can do it standing up, or sitting down. You can place your elbow on top of a table. Some people simply stand up and place their palms underneath the pendulum. It's up for you to decide which feels best.

* Give your pendulum a prayer, or invocation that says, "May I receive answers today for the highest good of all concerned." This will help you to understand yourself and the Universe better. I want to communicate only my subconscious mind. I welcome the help

from my spirit guides (or Angels -- whatever ethereal beings are you looking toward) to receive the answers and I need them." You can put this in words that resonate for your heart.

Holding Your Pendulum

As I mentioned above, you can position your pendulum as you find most comfortable. You must be able to hold your pendulum steady with one hand.

Now that you have purchased or made your pendulum, you need to train it. Your subconscious mind and yourself are "the boss." Your pendulum should be used as a divinatory tool.

To train your pendulum so it synchronizes with your subconscious brain, the first thing you need to do is hold the pendulum between your fingers. This can be done with your free hand or by placing your elbow onto a table (see the photos). Some people might wrap the string or the chain around a finger. However, the best method is to hold the pendulum between each of your first and third fingers.

Programming Your Pendulum

After you've completed your mental preparations, it's the time to program your pendulum. There are two possible methods. As the same method might not work for everyone. Try both to find the one that gives you the best answers.

A pendulum is available in five positions: clockwise or counterclockwise, up and down, left-and right, clockwise or still.

Method 1

This is your first interaction with your pendulum. You will ask it questions and it will answer them.

* Which motion would you use if you were to give a yes answer? The most common one is up-and–down. However, your pendulum could think differently. Keep the

pendulum still. Loudly speak. You can ask your pendulum to show you 'Yes' or to ask you a question. "Pendulum. Does my name X?" Your pendulum will then swing the opposite direction.

* Which motion would make you give a "No"? The most common choice is left-to–right. However, your pendulum could have other ideas. Now, hold the pendulum in place. Two methods can be used for determining a "No direction". You can ask your pendulum "Pendulum. Please show me a No." Or you can ask the pendulum questions that you already know the answers to. It's quite common to ask the pendulum the name and address of someone else for this portion of the programming. Your pendulum's direction will be "No"

* What would you like to see as a "Maybe?" response? Or counter clockwise. Let's speak loud. Ask the pendulum to give you the direction for "Maybe."

* What motion would make you want a "No response available at this moment" answer? It can be either counterclockwise or clockwise. This will give you the answer.

* The still-position -- Your pendulum should remain still and you should be able "Stop!"

Method 2

You will use the second method again to talk with your pendulum. But this time, you will tell it which way to go.

* What motion would get you a "Yes?" response? The most common answer is "Yes", but you can choose. Make sure to speak loud. Swing your pendulum in any direction you wish to answer "Yes". Speak "Pendulum", this is a way to say "Yes". Continue doing this for several times.

* What would you do for a no answer? The most popular is left-to - but that's up to your preference. Make sure to speak loud. To answer a "No", you must swing the pendulum in the same direction as your speech. As you continue to swing the pendulum in the desired direction, say "Pendulum".

* What motion would it be for a "Maybe?" Answer? Or counterclockwise. Use your voice to communicate. For a "Maybe", swing the pendulum as far as you wish. As you keep swinging your pendulum in the desired direction, say "Pendulum."

* What motion would make you want a "No answers available at the moment" answer? It can be either counterclockwise or clockwise. The motion that remains unused is the one you choose. Make sure to shout. For a "No Answer Available at This Time" answer, you can swing the pendulum any direction that you like. "Pendulum", this is the opposite of "No answer" and you can do this multiple times.

* The still-position -- You should tell your pendulum "Stop," to make it stay still.

Next -- Next, no matter what method you use to test it, let the pendulum learn the answers. Let it go through the motions. "Pendulum tell me 'Yes!' should get it moving the way you programmed. Then, repeat the procedure with the remaining commands. Keep at it until you see the pendulum responding to your programming. The pendulum can be tested by simply asking a question to which you already have the answer.

Caring for Your Pendulum

Your pendulum should not be left to anyone but you. Your pendulum comes programmed to your brain. You can only keep it useful by continually using it and "reminding it" of the way it responds to your subconscious direction.

Pendulums lose their ability sometimes to respond correctly. It could be caused by confusion, or someone else might have picked it. To fix this, place your pendulum in salt overnight. Then, reprogram it.

Phrasing Questions

You have successfully programmed your pendulum. Now what? This section will explain how to properly phrase questions for your pendulum.

A pendulum can only answer yes or no questions unless it is using a chart. The rest of this story will follow. Let's keep our focus on basic dowsing.

One of the most important skills to have when starting to dowse is how to phrase your question. This may seem obvious. However, the clearer your question is, the greater chance you'll get an exact answer. Be as specific as possible.

Before You Begin

It is important to hold the pendulum steady and repeat the invocation from up. This is exactly what you said before you programmed the pendulum. You should repeat it with each use.

Three Important Questions

Tradition has it that dowsers with experience will ask three questions prior to stating the main question.

"Can i?" -- this means, "Do i have the ability to answer this question?"

"May you?" -- this means "Do I have the right to answer the question?"

"Am-I-Ready?" refers to "Ams I prepared?"

Be sure to tell your pendulum to stop after you have asked a question.

This is a communication with both your subconscious and any other entities you have asked to help you get accurate answers.

What to do with vague responses?

If you get a "Maybe" or a "No answer at this time" reply to a question ask, rephrase the question. You might also try asking the question again if you do not receive an answer.

Ask your multiple pendulum owners if they have the right pendulum for that particular question. You can go through your entire collection before you find one that says "yes".

Consider taking a short break when all else fails and then asking the question later. Or, you could cleanse your pendulum.

Now you are able to use the pendulum to ask yes-or no questions. You can expect to achieve accurate results depending on how much effort and time you put into your pendulumwork. But you will now be equipped with the same skills that professional dowsers have.

Next, apply these fundamental skills to the investigation and analysis of your present, past, and future. Let's start!

Using Your Pendulum

We now know how we can buy or make a pedometer, how to hold it, how to write questions, and how program it. It's time to put these skills to work! This section will teach you how to analyze your present, future and past. Let's get started!

To Explore the past

The pendulum can be used by those who believe there is reincarnation to help them explore their past lives. While this exercise does not represent a complete Past Life Reveal, it can help to identify many of the lives that you might have had and teach you lessons. It is best to only look at one life per session. You can use a notebook to capture the information.

A typical past life session may look something like this:

* Choose a time for quiet reflection. If you'd like, you can dim the lights (but not so low that you can't clearly see your pendulum). A single candle can set the mood for a special occasion and alert your subconscious to it. You can also burn incense if that is what you prefer.

* Find a comfortable position and say a suitable prayers or invocations, such as this one: "May all the answers I receive today bring me greater understanding of myself and the Universe around us. I want to communicate only my subconscious mind. I welcome the help from my spirit guides (or Angels -- whatever ethereal beings you see) to find the answers I'm looking for.

* Take three deep, slow breathes. Now relax.

* Once you feel ready ask your pendulum some of the preparation questions. Next,

ask, "Am I ready for start?" Wait until it swings in the preprogrammed "Yes." direction.

Your pendulum will indicate that you are available for information. You can then begin your past life investigation by asking the question "Was this life more than 200 years ago?" Ask your pendulum the following question: "Was my life more then 200 years ago?" Then wait to see if it replies "Yes" or "No". If it does, continue asking "Was my life more over 300 years ago?". This will allow you to determine how long ago this particular life took. You can keep asking until your pendulum answers "Was this life more than 200 years ago?" and then wait to see if it responds with a "Yes" or a "No."

* Next is to identify the place where the life you are referring to took place. Ask your Pendulum, "Did the life in question take place in North America?". If so, wait for your answer. If you get a no, keep suggesting

more continents. If you get a no to all continents, it is possible that the life in question occurred in a galaxy other than the Milky Way. If that is true, you might want to use the alphabet table at the end this guide to spell out your planet's name. Because there are so much unknown names, don't be surprised that you don't recognize the planet's name. Now that you know the time and whereabouts of your past life, it is time to ask your pendulum whether or not you were a man.

* This is where you will learn even more about the past life. Ask your pendulum, "Was that me a member or the aristocracy?" and wait for its answer. If it says "No", indicate other sectors of society you may have been associated with, including merchant, soldier or worker. If you are not satisfied with any of the suggested occupations, you can ask the pendulum the alphabet chart for an answer. You can also ask about your past life, your children and

marriage. To complete this information, please click here

* The last question you should ask your pendulum concern the particular lesson you learned during that past life. The following are possible lessons that you might ask: love and emotion, wealth and success, as well as various physical problems such as poor health. This past life lesson may have given you clues about the current circumstances in your life.

Explore the Present

You can also use the same questioning technique used in the previous life pendulum sessions to explore questions that you may have regarding your current life. These questions can either be mundane, or esoteric.

Make the same preparations that you did before starting.

* You can try the technique by asking questions about what life lessons you should be paying attention to during this lifetime. Ask questions like "Is that my lesson for this lifetime to take better care my physical body?" or "Is that my lesson for this lifetime to be more patient?". Or any other personality traits you feel you are lacking. You can use an alphabet chart to spell things out.

* When you've identified a life lesson you need to pay closer attention to, ask specific questions. If you were able to answer "Yes" in the question "Is there a lesson I can learn from this life?" then you should dig deeper and ask questions about whether you need more exercise or a change of diet. Always consult a doctor before changing your routine.

* Common questions can be asked about current events in your life. Common questions address things such as money, career, love, and finances. If you suspect

your partner is cheating on you, first ask them if it is happening. Then, you can continue to ask about specific people.

A friend once questioned the pendulum about money that was hiding in her home. When the pendulum stated yes, she was overjoyed and kept asking for more information until it came down to her attic. There was a small jar filled with coins hidden in a corner. This yielded just $50. It was a disappointment but it was $50 more than she had previously.

To Explore the Future

You may be interested in programming your future by using a simple pendulum session.

This technique works in conjunction with the regular pendulum-session described earlier. It consists of four simple steps.

Step 1 -- Identify the Future You Desire. This step can be enjoyable -- it's almost similar to shopping in a cosmic store where only your imagination will limit you. This understanding allows you to set your goals for every aspect of your lives.

Step 2 - State your intention. It's important to state your intention loudly. It communicates to your subconscious mind that there is a desired outcome and you want it to happen. You can't make a plan for your life if you don't have one.

While you are stating your intention, keep your attention on your pendulum. This will cause it to respond in the "Yes!" motion. This action moves the intention from the mental realm into physical reality and signals to your subconscious that it is something you are serious.

Step 3 -- Visualize Your End Goal. Step 3 -- Visualize your Outcome. The most important aspect of visualization is to use your physical senses as much as possible.

Associating more of these sensations to your desired outcome makes it seem more real and more likely that you will be successful in creating the future you want. To give an example, imagine yourself living in Hawaii in a house at the beach. Take a moment to smell the aromas of the fragrant flowers. See the spectacular sunset.

Step 4 – Take Action. This is a crucial step as an intention that is not followed up with a plan of action will be a mere dream. If you can promise to do something every day, even though it may seem small, you will quickly realize your goal.

You can ask your future questions on a more basic level. For example, do you want to know what the future will hold for you?

To Contact Spirit

If you believe in an afterlife, where spirits visit this mortal world, you can use your pendulum to contact the dead.

For a pendulum, dress as usual. It helps to have a photograph of that person, or something similar. This will help you to visualize that person in your life and show your love for them. To help light the way, you might want to light a candle.

* You can also ask for positive, helpful spirits to attend your session.

A pendulum, if used properly, can be a powerful aid in an EVP(Electronic Voice Phenomena) session. You just need to turn on a Digital Recorder and let it run while you pendulum session. Next, listen to the recording.

I always talk to my "dearly deceased" and once, when trying to contact my brothers, I expressed my frustration at not being able to get any cooperation from the spirits. My question was "Does anybody hear me?" My pendulum was more responsive immediately. On the recording, I heard my brother say, "We hear X." It is a very rewarding moment.

Ask the following questions.

* Are there spirits who want to communicate or visit me?

* Is one spirit present? If you get a no, keep asking if it is two, three, or more. Until you get a "No", keep asking.

* Is X there? (Asking about an individual)

* Has X got a message for you?

You may have to go through many names before finding the one you want.

It can be tricky to decipher a person's message if you are not sure what it is. You might use the alphabet charts.

You can ask any question that you like. You might also want to ask if Y lives with X. (For example, does your grandmother live with a friend or relative? A pet that has passed?) If the spirit is happy and if there are any unfinished business. Again it may take a while before you figure this out. To find out a specific answer to your question, you should have "inside info" about any unfinished messages or business.

After your session has ended, be sure to thank the spirits for communicating. Your session is over.

This is how you can communicate with spirit guides. You use a combination question from the past lives instructions and spirit communication. What have your lessons been? Are there any messages from your spirit guide?

Other uses for a pendulum

Pendulums are used in dowsing for many reasons. For example, you could find lost objects.

You will need a map to show the location or a floor plan of the building if the object is inside. You do not need to create a floor plan. A simple drawing on paper will suffice. Ask the pendulum if it can point out the location. It will likely be necessary to ask additional yes/no questions to locate the exact location. The same techniques are used to locate water, minerals, and almost any other object.

How to use a pendulum for divination

Would you like to know how a pendulum works? Pendulums have a tremendous psychic power and I'm glad you asked. They can be used by your subconscious mind for secrets about yourself and your personality. These can be used to divinate the future and help with love magic or healing. They also serve to help you decide how to best move forward in order to achieve a specific goal.

A pendulum can be used to provide guidance. This is a way of asking for wisdom from within and beyond ourselves. This wisdom is something we are often unaware of but it is all around us, just waiting to be used. By asking your pendulum for help, you're literally opening up to a seemingly endless source of magical resources, a untapped data bank that holds incredible potential.

I strongly suggest that you purchase a pendulum. Pendulums are available in all sizes. Some people attach a personal item, such a key or locket, to a piece as a pendulum and then use that. Others prefer crystal pendulums and more sleek teardrop shaped ones, which can be made of metal or even glass.

I like to have a smooth bead made of glass on the end for a strong nylon yarn. The shape of my pendulum works best for me, as it spins with little resistance and feels light. Pendulums that feel too heavy can sometimes feel clumsy. A feather-light pendulum, on the other hand can have trouble spinning correctly. This can be corrected by a small amount of wind. The pendulum will almost call for you when it is properly balanced and aligned.

Don't worry about if you can't afford a brand new pendulum. In essence, a pendulum is just a weight at the end of a string. You can make your personal pendulum with a simple bead or a ring that is tied to a piece if cotton.

Do pendulums work?

Yes! Pendulums are very effective! Your subconscious mind is more aware than you are. Every day, it gathers many pieces of information. While there is not much space to retain and note everything, the information is still there deep within your mind.

Pendulums function because they bridge the gap between your conscious/subconscious mind. Pendulums enable you to bring deep submerged knowledge, sixth-sense style skills to the surface.

Your pendulum will swing, and your unconscious mind will not be able to notice, but your physical body will direct the swing to align it with the answer you have given. If you ask a pendulum a question, the answer will be based in psychic wisdom.

Pendulums can work. The best way to confirm this is to make one yourself.

Scroll down for the best method to use your pendulum for the very first time.

How to use the pendulum for maximum results

For best results, position your pendulum between your thumb, index, and thumb, keeping your elbow slightly bent. Relax at this stage. This allows the natural vibrations in your body to travel through the string and influence the pendulum's movement.

Don't get caught up in the details. Let go of all preconceived notions and thoughts. You can be detached. Don't worry about the answer you desire. Don't be afraid to trust the process. Just relax and wait patiently until your pendulum answers.

Ask your pendulum a question, and it will reply!

Remember that your pendulum can answer yes or no, depending on the direction of it's swing. Therefore, it is best not to ask questions you cannot answer by yes or zero. You can always drill deeper to find more specific answers. (e.g. "Will you fall in love with me this year?" -YES. "Will my love for someone I already like lead me to a new relationship?" YES. "Do I have a good knowledge of them at work?" NO. Etc.)

Sometimes you might see the pendulum swing erratically, in either a clockwise and anti-clockwise directions. This is usually best taken as a DON'T KNOW.

People love to do it again, whether they're able to formulate the question better or look at it from another angle.

How to interpret the pendulum

Your Pendulum can be easily read. Your pendulum's swinging clockwise or anticlockwise will determine whether you get a "yes" or "no" answer.

How do you decide which direction to go? I hear you cry! It can differ from person to person.

It's simple, just ask your pendulum! Keep it between your thumbs and fingers and let it swing gently, more like a pendulum spinning. The first question you should ask is:

"Is *insert your correct surname here* my name?"

Pay attention and wait patiently to see your pendulum go from spinning backwards or forwards to spinning in either an anticlockwise or clockwise direction. The pendulum will decide which direction it prefers and it will do so until the end.

TEST YOUR PENDULUM NOW. Prepare to be amazed. Ask your pendulum-

"Is Paddington Bear your name?"

Unless your pet has a rather furry personality or a marmalade addiction, I think your pendulum will say NO!

It's now time to ask some tough questions to your pendulum.

Pendulums may be used for divination and dowsing to discover water, metals and energy lines. It can also help you locate lost or ill people. These pendulums can be used as a guide to help you make good decisions in all areas of life. This includes giving advice on your romantic partner, making big decisions, such as moving house, and even helping you pick the perfect present. A pendulum is an amazing magical tool that can truly be invaluable!

Frequently Asked Questions about the use of pendulums

How to use your crystal pendulum

How to use crystal pendulums? Crystal pendulums should be used exactly the same as other pendulums. A crystal pendulum should be used exactly the same as any other. A pendulum that is made of beautiful lapis lazuli blue would be a good choice for someone who is interested in divination. This gem has a long-standing tradition of being valuable for its visionary qualities. Rose Quartz may be the best choice for a pendulum helping you make romantic decisions. Rose Quartz is strongly associated with love and healing.

RECAP – How to Use A Pendulum

Pendulums have many key functions and are an important magic tool.

* You can use the pendulum to predict your future or determine what the likely outcome is of a situation.

* A pendulum may be used to find water, minerals, or other ley energy lines.

*A pendulum is a tool that can be used to help you heal or diagnose yourself.

* A pendulum can also be used for advice regarding love or other matters in your life.

* You can use the pendulum to find knowledge you've forgotten, be it academic knowledge or your car keys.

* Some people claim they can use a pendulum to contact spirits, but that is a different topic altogether! (We'll save that for another day..).

How to Live a lucid Dream

How to Live a lucid Dream

Lucid Dreams - Have you ever heard of it? You may have tried one. Maybe you've ever had one, but are curious what the hell happened? This might be a new word for you, or an entirely different idea. In either case, it's awesome because you are about find out how to do something really amazing... To have adventures all night in your own brain!

What are Lucid Visions?

Lucid Dreams are dreams in which the dreamer is conscious that they are dreaming. This is a very fascinating experience. The dreamer is able to look at the dream with amusement, wonder about the details of the inner vision, and, in general, be completely astonished.

It is almost like a drug trip but with no risks. While everything appears and feels real, your mind knows that it's not. A lucid dream is a time when you can control everything.

As long as you remember the details, your first lucid nightmare will amaze you! You'll want to be able to do it again. You can train the mind to have amazing lucid fantasies at will.

How will I know when I have had my Lucid Dreams?

It is common to feel awe when you awake from your first lucid dreams. The dream you have in your head will show you that you 1) were aware you were dreaming; and 2) you probably looked at the wonderful scenes and events that your imagination had created in your virtual fantasy-world. Whatever is most comfortable for you!

Why are Lucid Dreams so useful to Wizards and Witches

Lucid Dreams are fun. Lucid Dreaming at will can be a wonderful gift that will stay with your whole life.

For the novice psychic, this is a safe method to allow your subconscious mind to work. While some people might be interested in mind-work, others may use psychedelic medication to test the mind's power. This is not the best way to go.

You'll find Lucid Dreaming a very useful tool in your psychic arsenal, as you become more adept and experienced witch/wizard/wizard. Our greatest tool is our imagination. A Lucid Dream allows us to use our imagination to achieve all of our psychic goals. It is one form of magical-work that is considered the best, and your psychic willpower could be extremely powerful if you use lucid dreams to back up your life.

Lucid Dreams can be used on a much higher level to predict your future and for other divination purposes. It can be used with higher energies as well as other people. For divination purposes, lucid dreams can be had by having a clear question or purpose in mind.

How to induce your self (Prepare your mind) to have a lucid dream

Many techniques are available to help the mind prepare for Lucid Dreaming. These are some of the most effective techniques that I have personally found.

1) Be aware that your dreams are important.

Many of us live our lives with little thought. When you become aware of your dreams, you can instill the belief that your subconscious mind is interested in what happens in your head at night. It then takes this information and adds meaning to them, making them more memorable. It is important to remember that only what you are focusing on will bring you results.

2) Establish the intention in your subconscious for a Lucid Dream.

This is easy. You can do this by repeating three times silently to yourself, "I'm going to have an amazing lucid dreams tonight, which will I clearly recall in the morning." Or something similar.

Write these words in your Dream Diary to add impact. Include a date next it. This will help you set the expectation of writing down the results every morning. Train your brain. Your mind should be able to anticipate what you are expecting from it.

3) Wakeful Mindfulness.

Your dreams are the mirror of your awake mind. Most people go about living their lives unaware and unaware of their real life.

To get yourself to wake up and realise that you are dreaming and to trigger a Lucid Dream you have to train your brain to question its reality. To stop and wonder "Is it real?" Am I dreaming or am I just lying?

It is possible to link this question with an ordinary physical event, which will train your mind subconsciously to contemplate this question several time per day, without ever having to ask.

Common physical events include checking your watch or phone, sitting down, using the toilet, and visiting the grocery or cooking. Mentally, ask yourself if you are seeing your watch or phone. Do you think I am dreaming?

4) Make a Dream Totem

This concept is similar with Wakeful Mindfulness. A Dream Totem, basically, is a tool to link an object in the real world to a thought. Your totem may be anything you like, such as a Rose Quartz Crystal crystal that you keep in a pocket or a ring.

This is how it works: hold your totem with one hand, multiple times per day. Then, say "am i dreaming?". Once you have done this enough, your totem will be brought out and associated with this dream. You'll be able immediately to notice that you are dreaming because you are actually dreaming.

Where can I go From Here?

Be patient. These strategies will work. They worked for my situation almost immediately. However, people are different. Some friends reported that they had difficulty seeing results for several weeks. This is why patience is important. You'll be glad you did!

A Dream Journal is useful. It's a way to keep track of all your dreams. Try to be as detailed as you can. Concentrate on how you felt about the events and your reactions.

Prepare to be amazed. Many times, I find that dreams have more meaning than they appear. They can also be very helpful tools after a second or third reading. If you feel that a particular dream is meaningful and pertains to a part of your life, keep returning to it to verify if it has begun to make sense.

Lucid Dreams are a tool that can help you live a happy, fulfilled life. Have fun, discover your true feelings, and unleash your potential!

The Art of Scrying- A Common Form of Magical Divination

Would it be possible to see the future ahead of you? To see the future and what fate may have in store for you if you continue on your current path. Would you like the opportunity to advise and help others? If you have some patience and perseverance you might try scrying.

Scrying is the art and science of fortune telling. One of the most well-known images of a gypsy fortune teller staring into a glass ball is a stereotypical one.

Magical Tools to Scry

To learn how to predict the future, divination students use several tools. These tools are easily accessible, and in the instance of a scrying visor, you can create your own at home. In just an hour you could be scrying by yourself.

Crystal Balls

Crystal balls are a widely used scrying tool. They are available online and look professional. Crystal balls are traditional but glass globes are cheaper and can be used for great results by beginners.

Use a crystal ball to meditate. Light a candle in front of it and look at the ball. The ball will help you relax your mind and create a meditative state. Give it time. It is important to focus on nothing other than the tranquility, peace, or serene crystal ball lit by candlelight. Your question should be brought up and any images that you might see will be taken into consideration.

Remember that you are using crystal ball to focus your attention. Images or ideas related to the question will not necessarily be visible upon the crystalball's surface. However, they may seem to just float into your mind. Notify your thoughts by paying attention to them.

Looking at mirrors

Scrying Mirrors traditionally have black, concave (curving downwards) mirrors. A scrying-mirror is usually placed face down on a desk. You place a candle on top and other objects around its perimeter in a circle. This will reflect back each other on the mirror's surface. Use the same method as the crystal ball to take notes of your ideas. For divination magic to succeed, don't stress out.

How to Make Your Own Scrying Mirror

You can also buy your scrying mirror online. It's much more affordable and, in my opinion, more efficient to make your very own. You will feel closer to your scrying mirror if you made it yourself.

Here is how to make an edifying mirror.

(You will need a transparent sheet of glass and black acrylic paint.

1. Clean the glass. Then, use your coloured markers (gold and/or silver) to create symbols around the edges. It doesn't make a difference what these symbols might be, as long they are significant to you. It could be Celtic symbol, Greek, Roman or Eygptian Gods/Deities, Numbers, or astrological signs. Do your research to make your scrying mirror an invaluable companion for divination magic. It will have a far greater impact than any product you can purchase in a shop.

2. When the symbols are dry, apply black paint to the entire back side of your scrying mirrored.

3. Mix together your dried herbs and make a powder. Then paint the back of the glass. The paint should dry before you apply a final coat. Now your scrying-mirror has three coats and is extremely black.

4. For the final touch to your scrying mirror and activation, you may want to consecrate the mirror and wash it with the full moon over night. Although this is not necessary, it can be a nice touch. To make it magically divinatory, you can place a charm on it.

5. It is customary to wrap your scrying-mirror in black silk, and keep it away from light when not in use. You are responsible for protecting your scrying mirror and keeping it safe from others.

When is the best moment to use divination magic, or scry?

Divination magic like scrying works best when performed at night, particularly during the new or full moon. However, don't let convention stop you from scrying at all. It is essential to ask the right questions, and to let your mind be open to new possibilities. Your mirror or crystal ball will help you focus in on the important things and allow your mind to drift off.

What incense or herbs should I light when I am chanting?

You can use herbs to stimulate the subconscious mind for divination. Some herbs are more difficult than others. Mugwort is very effective but you will need to order it from a specialty shop online. Parsley is more common than Frankincense but it's just as effective.

If you fail to find Mugwort, Parsley or Sage can be used instead. Wormwood and Mugwort will still work, however. Modern Witches or Wizards can get creative, and you might even find that you have a stronger affinity for Rosemary, Frankincense, or both.

Before you begin any divination and scrying sessions, make sure to cast a circle. You can then recite an easy divination charm.

"Open my vision,

Clear my sight

Bring the solution

"Into the light!"

- Selene Silverwind

How to learn remote viewing - A layman's guide

Did you realize that your mind powers are capable of traveling anywhere in the universe! To locate hidden secrets and find things over vast distances. Remote Viewing can allow you to do all this and more.

They are not only possible, they also require no latent psychic skill or special skills - they just require patience, practice, and adherence a specific formula, as established by the CIA in 1973.

Be patient with me. I don't expect to be able accept all the above without more explanation. It is not clear how Remote Viewing works. However, it is a concept that was studied by the CIA back in 1970. Project Stargate revealed surprising results. (If you are interested in reading the declassified documents describing these experiments in more detail, please refer to https://www.cia.gov/library/readingroom/docs/CIA-RDP96-00789R003300210001-2.pdf)

Consider it. If the CIA (a serious and important department in government) was willing to fund research on Remote Viewing's potential applications for use during wartime spying, surveillance, and the like, then there must have been some evidence that Remote Viewing is a real phenomenon. Remote Viewing is a wonderful tool that can enhance and improve the quality of your life.

What exactly is remote view?

Remote viewing allows you to tap into your subconscious mind to obtain information about difficult targets. These targets could be people, places or things. While some might call these abilities "psychic" or even "psi," it is a gross underestimation of Remote Viewing. It is actually a scientifically formulated skill which can produce consistent results in laboratory conditions, with accuracy of up to 80 percent. Remote Viewing, as far I know, is a complex process that no one understands. However, it isn't just mumbo-jumbo.

It was only recently that we all understood the basics of ball lightening. The tension created by ball lightning's surface was called by the CIA "an unexplainable phenomenon according to current laws of physics". NASA is using these previously unexplained properties of the ball lightning to help in its development of the Fusion Propulsion Rocket Engine. This engine has the potential for greater speeds than we have ever seen, and it can be used to send us to Mars in 30 - 45 Days. But, just because something is not explained does not necessarily mean it does not exist. We need to be open-minded, witches/wizards. However, not so open-minded that our brains are ruined.

Remote Viewing: A Fascinating History

Operation Stargate is a top secret programme the CIA developed back in the 1970's. This was to explore how the human mind can acquire data on a subconscious scale. This subject was the subject to years of secret scientific research with the help of people like Uri Gellar. Through top secret government funding, a protocol was created that could improve the unconscious process of data collection. This program reached remote viewing accuracy levels well beyond what was expected. Remote Viewers were also able to accurately predict the location of key Cold War storage facilities.

Remote Viewing: The Mechanisms

The stranger the world becomes, the more we learn about it. Quantum Physicists are sure to agree! Remote Viewing operates on the basis that all of the universe is made up of information, or a matrix. Remote Viewing can be described as tapping into this interweaving, or matrix, of time and reality. It allows you to unpick the threads in the universe. A universe that is infinitely possible and timeless.

In this reality, our common sense notions concerning cause and effects and therefore time or space cease to be meaningful when everything is reduced to the quantum level. A level at which the very fabric of our reality is only waves. Based solely on probabilities, waves can appear and vanish, but they do exist. You cannot say that anything is "real". It is impossible to know. Remote Viewing is found in that thrilling space between the familiar and the unknown. Today it seems magical, tomorrow it might be science fact.

Remote Viewing, which is a structured and teachable skill, does not require any aptitude or latent psychic talent. Remote Viewing does not require any special abilities or latent psychic ability. It is available to all who wish to be a wizard or witch. It will be easy to master if you are patient and take your time.

To initiate a Remote Viewing session as described by the CIA you will first need to locate your "cue" - the question to which the CIA has provided a guideline. These cues can include everything from the location and timing of the next catastrophe to the nature and character of your bankcard. Layman's way, it means that you have to identify exactly what you would like to discover in your remote viewing session. It may be helpful to write this down.

Remote viewing targets are usually described pictorially. Draw what you think that you have seen.

It is important to resist the urge to write it down immediately. Because the subconscious works through images or sensations first, words will come later. Also, once the perception has words attached, it will become more concrete than you would like. Give yourself room for flexibility. You can see grey walls, darkness. Do you live in a prison or a cave on the beach? Too much emphasis on the subjective reality can lead to misunderstandings. It is the objective reality you desire to record.

Although you may not achieve perfection in the first attempt, have faith that you will make improvements each time. Confidence is key; you'll be amazed!

How to Astral Project

Would you like to know more about the astral project? You have reached the right place. You have come to the right spot! This experience can be used for divination or as a part of your spells.

First, you need to understand what Astral Project or an Out of Body Experience is if you want to learn more about how to Astral Project. To do this, we need to travel back in history and examine the practices of Yoga & Meditation.

Many Ancient Cultures believe in the existence of etheric energies bodies. This means our (fabulous!) physical body is just one entity. pan dimensional soul. These beliefs may take many forms that can encompass a wide range of religions and philosophical systems. A branch of Yoga called Kundalini Yoga acknowledges the existence 10 etheric energy body. In ancient Egyptian mythology, it was thought that the physical human body was just temporary residence for the Ka, or human life force, as well as the Ba, or soul. Shamanism is known for its long-held belief, dating back thousands of year, that the Shaman can astral travel - allowing them to leave their bodies to communicate with their ancestors and spirits.

These cultural ideas, and philosophies, differ in many small details. But the fascinating thing about all of them is that they all share the same thread - that it is possible to have the etheric layer of a complete individual be separated forcibly or through force of will. This would cause an out of body experience or astral projection.

Astral Projection: A sometimes Divisive Subject

What exactly does Astral Projection mean?

If you want to learn how to astralproject, every student will want to find out exactly what it's all about! The astral projection will require that you know where your soul or consciousness is going when it happens. This is an important consideration to make before you start. Philosophers have debated this question for centuries.

There are two major theories that surround astral projection. These two theories can be summarised as The Phasing Model/The Mystical Model. They address the issue of whether astral projecting is an actual, physical journey or just an inner journey through different phases.

The Phasing Model, as proposed by Robert Monroe, describes an astral projected as a passing, or phasing, through another plane. They tune in and change channels, just like a radio. This idea is related the traditional philosophy that reality cannot exist and is created instead by thought or consciousness.

The Mystical Model contains many beliefs, each with its own uniqueness. However, what unites these belief systems is the notion that astral projecting is a real journey by the human consciousness. The consciousness, or spirit, is carried beyond the body and travels via an etheric "energy" body.

Whatever your preference, you will find that it is exciting and enlightening, no matter which model.

Is Astral Projection Dangerous?

Popular culture tends to make it easy for people to call the unknown or any phenomena that isn't explained as normal dangerous. Many people have heard horror stories that astral projection can lead to permanent death or disconnection from the body. You may also hear that it is possible to lose control of your body and become lost in spirit realms. Wandering, presumably, forever...Sob! It would be like forgetting the location of your body when you go on vacation - it just isn't happening!

Although this sounds romantic, it is not true. They are actually a knee-jerk reaction to the superstitious and ignorant masses. You can ignore this and continue your astral projection practice to your heart's delight!

As with any other meditational technique, it is best to practice your astral projection somewhere quiet and peaceful where you won't be disturbed. This is not to cause you to be rudely or rapidly awakened from others when you are deeply in a relaxed mental condition.

History Of Pendulum

A pendulum may be described as a weighted and symmetrical object, normally suspended from one cord or chain. Although it is crystallized, it is not made of any magnetic material. The pendulum works as both an information transmitter and receiver. It responds by moving in different directions. Pendulum history goes back to the early 1600s. Galilei Galileo found it and it was first used for timekeeping. It was used to keep time until the 1930s, when it became the most precise in the universe. Pendulums may be used for divination or dowsing purposes.

Galilei Galileo an Italian scientist, researched the different qualities and properties of pendulums. He discovered a key property that makes these pendulums very useful and vital in time keeping. This property was called isochronism. He discovered that a pendulum's duration is almost independent of the width or amplitude of one swing. He also discovered the pendulums' period is not dependent on the bobs mass but directly compares to the square root the pendulums length.

One of the earliest documented uses of a pendulum is in the first century's seismometer. This was the device of Heng Zhu, a Chinese scientist. After it was shaken by an earthquake, the device activated levers and swayed. Heng would then let loose a very small ball-shaped sphere from the metal device. The ball fell into one the eight mouths of the metal toads beneath the device after it was released by one the levers. This signalled the direction from which the earthquake was taking place.

Pendulum was once used for divination, dowsing, and dowsing. Cameron Verne was an American pendulist who was invited by South Africa's government during the Cold-

War era in the late 1960s. He was to use his pendulum to help the nation trace precious natural assets. The United States of America government denied him his passport. Before, he had already demonstrated his skills in dowsing and was able locate on the map all United States Navy submarines. Later, Cameron was declared a national security-risk by the CIA of America and was prohibited from leaving the United States.

It is worth noting that, throughout history, people have used a pendulum as an indicator of direction and especially when their lives were in danger. During Vietnam-war, almost all of the United States Marines were trained in underground-mine and underground tunnel tracing. Merrylees Kenneth got a contract as the country's bomb-detection expert during the second war. He was able, thanks to his unique dowsing techniques, to locate bombs that had delayed action fuses and had entered underground.

In conclusion, it's important to highlight the most significant areas where dowsing is used historically. It was highly appreciated for its ability at locating and tracing oil, gold, and water. Pendulum use to locate mines is a method that many countries used to benefit greatly from their minerals. France is one example.

Choosing Your Pendulum

The pendulum is the most widely used tool for divination, dowsing, and dowsing. The pendulum's use is easy to learn. The pendulum must be suitable for your body, size and desired color so that you can quickly learn how it works. The pendulum may be made from metal, wood, or even crystal stones. The pendulum's characteristics will change depending on the material used. A pendulum made of metal has a smooth feeling, but is heavier, giving the divination period a feeling balance.

Where can I use it?

The purpose of your pendulum choice will be determined by what you intend to use it for. There are many different ways that you can use the Pendulum. First, it can be used to locate water lines. This is where you might consider a pendulum made out of metal. This is because it will give your sense of balance.

Is it possible to choose a pendulum to help find a lost pet or object? A wood pendulum will work well because it is lightweight and easy to locate the lost objects. Pendulum can also help you divinate the future. A pendulum can help you identify allergic reactions. A pendulum is also a good choice to help with negativity removal and cleansing. If you are a beginner, it is important to ask the question: Why do I need the pendulum? You'll be able select the right pendulum to suit your needs.

Personal taste

It is clear that no pendulum works better than the others. This idea is important to keep in mind when choosing your pendulum. This will allow you to pick the right pendulum for you. It is important to choose one that will respond to your energies. Try a variety of options to ensure that the best is chosen for you.

What kind do I need for my pendulum?

You can choose from many different pendulums for divination. For the best results, however, you do not need to purchase a high-end pendulum. The type of pendulum that you choose depends on your preference. People often consider the crystal pendulum to be associated with clarity. It is also associated in higher purpose.

The amethyst type is the other, and it is associated strong with spirit connection. It also has the tranquilizing qualities of a Rose Quartz crystal. You can use this pendulum to build strong spiritual connections. Start with one type of pendulum and then work your way up to the others.

You should make sure that you charge your energy and clean the pendulum before you start using it. To cleanse it, you can keep your pendulum out for drowsing in direct sunlight for one day. Hold it in your hands for 15 minutes and then ask your angels for assistance.

Programming Your Pendulum

Programming your Pendulum is a difficult process that requires extreme dedication.

Pendulums have one thing in common: they can answer any question you ask, as long as the answer is either YES OR NO. It is essential to define the exact meaning for each movement of the pendulum.

Below is an overview of what it takes to program a pendulum.

- First, pick a suitable location to seat in for the process.

- With your elbow resting on your desk, place your feet flatten on the floor.

- Carefully support your pendulum using one hand. The other is between your thumb or index finger.

- Allow your energy to flow freely but not for accuracy. Instead, straighten your head and spine.

- Now, place the other hand straight on to the table.

Relax and take a deep breath. You can then relax and take a deep breath.

Eliminate any object, thought, emotion, or other thing that may cause a problem during the remainder of the process. It is a good idea not to feel fatigued when using a pendulum.

Next, ask your pendulum the following key questions.

The pendulum is able to move in a circle, left-right, or up-down. For him to know his YES and No, he will need to do this exercise multiple times over a minimum of one week. You will find that NO answers rarely differ from the above. You can always test it. However, you do not need to change it.

If you want to test the pendulum's accuracy, ask it a clear question. If you want to know your sex type, your pendulum could answer the following question: "Am I a man?" In this example, I am male. Therefore, if my pendulum says NO and I am still a boy, I must continue the process with similar questions until I feel 100% confident that my pendulum is correct.

Ingram Content Group UK Ltd.
Milton Keynes UK
UKHW021119180423
420361UK00014B/982